Building Competence in Business Administration

A TEXT FOR NVQ LEVEL II

Texts for NVQ written by Sheila May and published by Stanley Thornes:

Level 1: Foundation Competences in Business Administration
Level 2: Building Competence in Business Administration
Level 3: Building Secretarial Competence

Building Competence in Business Administration

A TEXT FOR NVQ LEVEL II

Sheila May

Stanley Thornes (Publishers) Ltd

First published in 1991 by:
Stanley Thornes (Publishers) Ltd
Old Station Drive
Leckhampton
CHELTENHAM GL53 0DN
England

British Library Cataloguing in Publication Data

May, Sheila
    Building competence in business administration:
    A text for NVQ level II. — (Business
    administration)
    I. Title   II. Series
    658

    ISBN 0-7487-1277-1

Acknowledgement

The author wishes to acknowledge the support role of Raymond May, whose assistance in a variety of tasks would otherwise pass unrecorded.

Typeset by Tech-Set, Gateshead, Tyne & Wear.
Printed and bound in Great Britain at The Bath Press, Avon.

Contents

Foreword

The work of the Council for National Vocational Qualifications has progressed significantly in the past year, and its work has been assisted by publications like Sheila May's text for the Level 1 NVQ in Business Administration, *Foundation Competences in Business Administration*. Now we have the continuation volume, *Building Competence in Business Administration*, to take trainees through NVQ Level 2. There are three routes currently available at Level 2, enabling trainees to specialise in administration, finance or the secretarial function, and all three options are covered in this volume. The context of work has moved up a gear, as is appropriate for Level 2, which is defined in NCVQ's National Framework as accrediting 'competence in a significant range of varied work activities, performed in a variety of contexts. Some of the activities are complex or non-routine, and there is some individual responsibility or autonomy. Collaboration with others, perhaps through membership of a work group or team, may often be a requirement.' The activities set out in this volume match that specification.

Sheila May's first volume has been successful, and I am confident that this continuation work will also enjoy success. Most of all, however, I am confident that those in training will achieve success by applying themselves conscientiously to the business situations set out for them in these pages.

Ernest Lee
LCCIEB, 1991

Introduction

If you want to obtain a nationally-recognised qualification in business administration you will find that this book will help you. It is suitable for full-time college students, trainees in Employment training and Youth training schemes, those already working in the field of business administration and others wishing to do so.

This book helps to promote the competences required in two ways. Firstly, through a text which includes procedures, advice, lists and general rules against which routines can be checked; and secondly through a series of tasks for personal competence building which integrate and reinforce the content of the text and provide opportunities for efficient learning through active involvement.

A common thread of knowledge and skills runs through clerical work, but the setting in which you have to carry out the work and the detail and content of the daily routine vary greatly. This book deals with common knowledge and skills in the text, and provides for individual circumstances in the Competence Builders which take account of your own training or work situation. In this way, a variety of readers with differing degrees of experience and responsibility are catered for.

COMPETENCE BUILDERS

Many of the Competence Builders specify the type of work to be carried out, but require you to negotiate opportunities for doing so. These can be discussed with your boss or tutor. Any tasks in which competence is already proven can be ignored. Since locating, abstracting and presenting information are skills in which you are required to build up competence, you will find that readily-available facts are not always given in the book, but deliberately left for you to find out. Where information has to be obtained, this should be used as an opportunity for practising note-taking skills if you have them. Some material for typing should be recorded, in order to provide audio-typing practice, where this is appropriate.

The Competence Builders are useful for another reason: the work produced will result in an individual file of material which you can use and add to for personal reference. The checklists in this book can be personalised, typed and added to your file, together with appropriate leaflets, instructions and other such information. The file can be paper or computer-based, or a combination, depending on your own circumstances. Amended and kept up-to-date as the need arises, it will continue to be a valuable resource for a long time to come and one which is relevant to your workplace.

The term 'organisation' in the Competence Builders refers to your working or studying environment, whether this is a firm or company, a college or a training organisation. The Competence Builders can be carried out in a real situation or realistic simulation. Real situations are best and if you are in college then work experience might offer opportunities to carry out some of the Competence Builders. Making contact with someone working in business administration who would be willing to act as a mentor and be prepared to discuss work done on the Competence Builders is also most helpful to a full-time student.

Where appropriate and/or more convenient, individual Competence Builders can be undertaken as group projects. In this way, you will develop group skills as well as the skills specific to the task.

Working through the Competence Builders will provide you with practice, and in some cases actual material, for assessment of your competence. Assessment by others provides an important recognition that what you are doing is correct and it is necessary when seeking a qualification. Equally important is self-assessment, since for much of your working life you will have to judge for yourself whether or not what you have done is satisfactory. For this reason, many of the Competence Builders ask you to assess your own work and qualities.

QUALIFICATIONS

As you will appreciate, qualifications are important, particularly when job-seeking. Courses leading to traditional qualifications offered by examining bodies have long been available. Many still are and anyone studying for them will find this book, together with a review of past examination questions, a useful means of preparation.

National Vocational Qualifications (NVQs) are approved by the National Council for Vocational Qualifications and are gaining in importance. These are awarded for competent performance in work activities to the standards required in employment. Where possible, assessment is carried out in the workplace, but can take place in a realistic, simulated environment. The industry-led body responsible for drawing up the standards has stated that 'Assessment of an individual's performance should be based upon situations which require demonstration of competence, requiring a combination of skills and related knowledge, in purposeful and recognisable tasks. It is the successful, day-to-day, consistent demonstration of competence, which is of prime importance in determining that occupational competence has been achieved . . .'. Anyone carrying out assessment must be recognised as competent to do so by the awarding body, for example, The London Chamber of Commerce Examinations Board, City & Guilds of London Institute, Pitman Examinations Institute, RSA Examinations Board or Business & Technician Education Council (BTEC).

NVQs are awarded at a number of levels, the first three being defined as follows:

▶ Level I recognises competence in the performance of a range of work activities which are primarily routine and predictable, or provide a broad foundation, primarily as a basis for progression.

▶ Level II recognises competence in a broader and more demanding range of work activities, involving greater individual responsibility and autonomy than at Level I.

▶ Level III recognises competence in skilled areas that involve performance of a broad range of work activities, including many which are complex and non-routine. In some areas, supervisory competence may be a requirement at this level.

Credit can be given for parts of NVQs, called units. This means that you can build up a qualification over a period of time, and at a pace to suit your own needs and circumstances. You can work for units at different levels simultaneously, thus allowing for greater expertise in specialist areas to be accredited.

Should you wish to gain an NVQ there are no barriers such as age, or where and how competence was acquired. There is no requirement that NVQ candidates must have followed any particular type of course or training programme before undertaking assessment for the qualification. Therefore, anyone can reach competence through on-the-job training, experience, college courses, distance learning, private study or a combination of these.

The text and Competence Builders in this book cover the requirements of the Level II Business Administration National Vocational Qualification Units. Only certain of these units are compulsory and there is a choice of the others according to whether you wish to take the administration, secretarial or financial route to the award. Appendix I shows compulsory units and the choices available from the rest. Appendix II shows how the Units in this book relate to each of the NVQ units.

In Appendix II you will notice that the units are subdivided into what are called 'Elements of competence'. In each of the Competence Builders in this book, the main elements that the tasks help you to become competent in are indicated. These numbers will also help you in keeping a record of what you have achieved and you could use Appendix II as a checklist for this purpose.

Finally, do not stop when you have achieved your Level II qualification. Remember, as you progress in your career you will acquire new competences which can be assessed and credited in units under the NVQ system. You can, therefore, work at your own pace towards a Level III award – and beyond.

Creating and Maintaining Business Relationships

Effective human relationships are essential in business. Whether you like or dislike people you have to create and maintain professional relationships with them. Your attitudes and their attitudes influence these relationships, and the more you are aware of this the more allowances you can make.

Essential personal qualities include knowing and being yourself; but knowing yourself is not easy. It means thinking about what you say and do, and questioning why you behave in a particular way. It means thinking about difficult situations you have been in, recalling what was said and done, and trying to determine how responsible you were for what happened. For example, why was somebody angry? Was it because of what you said, the tone of your voice or the manner you adopted? Think equally about the contributions you made to good situations, ones in which everyone went away satisfied with the outcome.

Being yourself is complicated because you are unlikely to be the same all the time. In thinking about this you will probably find that you differ according to who you are with and the situation you are in. This is not being insincere, it is showing flexibility, which is necessary in handling human relationships. Being yourself includes continuing to maintain your personal sense of values, but at the same time adapting things like your choice of language and speech patterns, according to your awareness of other people's temperaments, the positions they hold and the position you hold in relation to them.

Recognise that people have moods. These are determined by factors, such as the time of day (some people are at their best in the morning while others do better in the evening), by their state of health and by what has already happened that day. Allow for this in other people and also learn to recognise what affects you.

Competence Builder 1   *(Elements 10.1, 10.2 and throughout)*

Consider your work/college relationships. Could any be improved? To help you do this, keep a diary of 'difficult' encounters with people; situations where you felt uncomfortable, angry or irritated, or where you had to work very hard to achieve a satisfactory conclusion. Reflect on each one and note down anything you could have done to have improved matters. After a while, you should discover those who have 'funny little ways' whom you will have to tolerate. Be more aware of your own approach and manner, and the ways in which you can make improvements.

In doing this, you should find that you are becoming more sensitive to other people's moods and manner, and this will improve your own effectiveness. If there is anyone with whom you can discuss, comfortably and frankly, the situations you have noted, you will find this extremely helpful.

PROFESSIONAL RELATIONSHIPS WITH OTHER MEMBERS OF STAFF

People's appearance affects the way in which others respond to them. Similarly, their general attitude and show of interest also affects response. Think how difficult it is to talk to someone who appears dull or bored.

Competence Builder 2   *(Elements 10.1, 10.2 and throughout)*

Consider the image that you present:

▶ What do you look like? Are you well-groomed and appropriately dressed (see page 67)? Do you conform to your organisation's standards for dress and appearance?

▶ What is your general attitude? Are you cheerful, polite and good tempered?

▶ How do you respond to people? Are you interested and alert?

If you have anyone who can be relied upon for constructive criticism, discuss these factors with that person. Set yourself target dates for achieving identified improvements.

It is easier to get on with people when you know them. Over a period of time, if you are observant, you will recognise people's peculiarities and so be able to make allowances for them. Be careful though. It is easier to see others' faults and failings than it is your own. You must allow for the fact that the way in which people behave towards you is affected by the way in which you behave towards them. It is also easier to excuse your own mistakes, especially if you have a reason, such as feeling unwell. You must recognise that this happens and similarly be prepared to excuse others.

The length of time it takes to get to know your colleagues will vary. They may come from different backgrounds, have differing viewpoints and the age range might be wider than expected. The work situation brings together people with a wide range of talents, experience and interests; people who might not otherwise have much in common. Do not let such differences become barriers, and remember that getting to know people does not necessarily imply becoming friends. You may indeed find someone with whom you can become friendly, although it is wise to take things steady before becoming too involved. It is not easy to cool or drop an unsatisfactory friendship if it is with a close work colleague.

The relationships you are called upon to create and maintain at work are likely to be with colleagues at different levels. In establishing your relationships bear in mind that it is always a mistake to be servile to superiors or to talk down to subordinates. People at work are interdependent, regardless of their positions, and this is something which must be sustained if work is to progress smoothly. This requires that everyone must respect other people's roles within the organisation and recognise the responsibilities each one carries for getting the work done.

In order to be effective you will find yourself dependent on certain colleagues, for example to provide you with specific information. They must feel that they can trust you and thus being discreet is important. Refuse to listen to, or repeat, office gossip, scandal and rumour. Combine this with being tactful, friendly, cheerful and using your common sense. Above all, never forget that competence in a job depends on maintaining relationships as well as on technical competence.

Your colleagues will equally be dependent upon you. Any requests made of you (provided the carrying out of them comes within your area of responsibility) should be dealt with promptly and willingly. Essential information should be passed on without delay. Ensure that this is always accurate, and thus build up a reputation for yourself of being reliable.

Do not be afraid to ask for assistance when in doubt. It is better to seek help than to carry on making errors through ignorance. No one minds helping, provided requests are made politely, are not demands, are not constant, and that requests for the same information are not made over and over again.

Competence Builder 3   *(Elements 10.1, 15.1 and throughout)*

You must be aware of your own and your employer's legal responsibilities under the Health and Safety at Work Act, and you may need to refer problems which arise regarding the Act.

As background information, check your knowledge of the Act. Check also that you know the person whom you should refer to with any problems regarding the Act and its implementation.

Sometimes you will need to negotiate with your colleagues how you divide work and responsibilities between you. Aim to make arrangements which will be mutually beneficial, as well as work effectively, and so satisfy everyone concerned. Should you find that you encounter significant difficulties in making these arrangements, or indeed in any other aspect of your working relationships, then first try to resolve the problems by discussion with the person(s) concerned. If these discussions fail, then you must report the matter accurately to the appropriate person in authority, for resolution.

Competence Builder 4

(Elements 10.1 and throughout)

a) Discuss with your boss or tutor, or as a group exercise with fellow trainees or students, the types of working-relationship difficulties which might need to be referred to a higher authority. Are there ways in which they could be resolved without such help?

b) Find out, and keep a note of, to whom you should refer different types of relationship difficulties which you might not be able to resolve yourself, and any procedures you would be required to follow.

c) Keep a log, for discussion with your assessor, of occasions when you feel that you have shown yourself to be competent in creating and maintaining professional relationships with other members of staff.

PROFESSIONAL RELATIONSHIPS WITH CUSTOMERS AND CLIENTS

At various stages during your working life, you are likely to be meeting customers and clients, and this imposes certain obligations on you. For example, it is very important that you convey a good impression of your organisation (see pages 66–8). How you look, speak and behave, will all play a part. This should accord with your role at work, since people are disconcerted when someone differs widely from the appearance and behaviour that is expected of their role. As an office worker you need to know not only what an office worker does, but how people expect you to look and behave.

People arriving at your place of work should be greeted promptly and politely, and those known should be greeted by name in an appropriate and friendly manner. In most cases, you can expect to obtain a similar response. This may not happen if a customer/client has called to make a complaint, but by being pleasant you might succeed in taking the edge off some of the irritation.

When greeting visitors, aim to convey the impression that you are pleased to see them and are prepared to help, so that they can expect to go away satisfied. Be friendly and show your willingness, but avoid giving an impression that you are available for a 'good old chat'. Although you should give your full attention in an obvious manner, because this promotes goodwill and trust, and it is impolite to do otherwise, you have to take into account other work to be dealt with and the needs of other customers/clients.

Competence includes being careful not to disclose confidential information since this can seriously damage your organisation; knowing where to find information (see pages 15–18); and well-developed conversational skills which you can use to make your professional relationships increasingly effective.

Competence Builder 5 *(Elements 10.2, 11.1, 11.2, 12.2, 14.1, 15.1, 15.2, 21.1, 21.2, 22.3)*

a) Check that you are using the correct greeting styles for your organisation.

b) Make a note of your organisation's policy on disclosure of information and always adhere to this.

c) Discuss with your boss or tutor what you need to be aware of regarding your organisation's obligations to the public, for example, features of Public Liability and the Trade Descriptions Act. Where relevant, find out and photocopy, or type up, reference notes for yourself.

CONVERSATIONAL SKILLS

When you speak to someone face-to-face you have several means of conveying information apart from words; by the tone of your voice, your facial expressions and gestures. You can use these to reinforce your words, soften their meaning or even convey the opposite impression to that given by the words alone. If this sounds impossible just think of the different ways in which the simple words 'Don't do that' can be expressed.

Oral communication is immediate. It allows for reactions and understanding to be checked on the spot, discussion to take place and decisions to be reached without delay. This appears to be very advantageous, but there are disadvantages. Because spoken words are more spontaneous than written ones they may not be as accurate in their meaning. The words you choose may be emotionally laden, as may those used by the respondent. There is also the disadvantage that you have no permanent record to which you could refer or put before someone else. This can be particularly important in the case of a complaint.

The difficulties which can be experienced in face-to-face encounters underline the importance of your recognising immediately when your own knowledge and job responsibilities are being exceeded. In these cases, you should immediately refer the customer/client to an appropriate person to deal with the matter. The way in which you do this should maintain your credibility to deal with other matters on future occasions and must not give the impression that the organisation has incapable staff.

Speaking

It is important to recognise that judgements are made about people and, therefore, about organisations, as a result of what is said and the way in which it is said. Speech can offend and irritate, and getting out of trouble (or not into it in the first place) is a skill you should develop. Tactical points which may help include the following:

▶ If you know in advance that you are going to have a difficult situation to deal with rehearse in your mind what might be said to you and what you might say. Plan ahead.

▶ Be obviously sincere.

▶ Let other people state what they have to say without interruption.

▶ Do not be abusive, or rude in any other way.

▶ Remain calm against all provocation and do not raise your voice.

▶ Be prepared to compromise or give way over unimportant matters.

▶ Think before speaking. Even face-to-face there is time to do so.

▶ Be responsive to signs, such as yawning or looking at a watch, which indicate that the other person has listened long enough.

▶ Be responsive to signs, such as frowning, which might indicate that the listener has not understood.

▶ Be aware of other effects that you are having on your listener, for example, causing anger or anxiety, and seek to overcome these reactions by modifying what you are saying or giving further explanation.

▶ Do not repeat yourself unless it is done deliberately for emphasis.

▶ Do not be apologetic for stating a point of view. Keep apologies for occasions when this is appropriate, for example, in order to put right any harm done to the customer/client.

▶ Do sound interested, alert and enthusiastic, when appropriate.

▶ Avoid fiddling with jewellery, jiggling coins in your pocket, etc.

▶ Allow others an opportunity to escape from difficult situations and save face when they have made a mistake.

Some people find it difficult to speak clearly. Lack of confidence can play a role in this, so if you have problems bolster your confidence by being competent and well-prepared. Seek also to improve your way of speaking. Here are some pointers:

▶ Look directly at the person to whom you are speaking.

▶ Do not hold your hand in front of your mouth.

▶ Do not speak so quickly that the words are too fast for the listener to take them in, or they come out in a jumble.

▶ Do not speak so slowly or laboriously that the other person's mind is encouraged to wander.

▶ Avoid 'ums', 'ers' and repeated phrases, such as 'You know what I mean'.

▶ Do not speak so quietly that you cannot be heard or so loudly that you can be heard some distance away.

▶ Use your lips to articulate words properly and avoid mumbling.

Overall, try to make your speech easy and interesting to listen to by introducing variety. Vary the volume so that some parts are louder or softer than others. Vary the tone to add emphasis to the feelings you wish to convey. Vary the pace, which also emphasises and gives extra meaning to the words you choose.

Competence Builder 6 *(Elements 10.1, 10.2, 11.1, 11.2, 12.2, 14.1, 14.2, 15.1, 15.2, 19.1 and throughout)*

Carefully consider the tips given above. Think hard and critically about your own speaking performance. Identify any problems you recognise and make an effort to eliminate them. Practising should help you to improve, but first you have to be brutally honest with yourself in order to determine where improvements can be made. Additionally, consult a friend or colleague whom you trust to make constructive criticism.

Listening

Listening is not given the attention it needs, possibly because it seems to come so naturally, but this is deceptive. Listening requires active participation. You choose whether or not to listen. Because the process is a conscious one it is possible to block out unwanted noise in order to concentrate on other matters or sounds. It also helps to explain why people do not remember names and arrangements; they may simply not have listened hard enough.

As you have control over your listening it is something you can improve. You should also find that an improvement in your ability to listen is accompanied by an improvement in your other conversational skills. This is because you will have picked up much more from the other person and have, therefore, much more to respond to. So what can be done to improve your listening skills?

▶ Be prepared to put effort into listening. Remember that it is something you have to do actively, not something which you accept passively.

▶ Tune in quickly. Do this by relating what the speaker is talking about to your previous knowledge.

▶ Concentrate on the speaker, on what is being said, and on facial expressions, since these can add to, or detract from, the words, and confirm or oppose what is being said.

▶ Listen out for what is important to the speaker because these will be primary matters that you must give attention to.

▶ Try to determine what the person is seeking to achieve by the conversation. Is your objective likely to be the same?

▶ Ask for something to be repeated if you have not heard clearly, but be careful, this can be irritating if done too often.

▶ If necessary, ask for clarification to aid your understanding of what has been said.

▶ Encourage the speaker to state all that is necessary by giving good feedback. If you look bored or long-suffering you may cause the speaker to curtail what is being said, leaving you without all the information necessary to deal with the matter.

▶ Do not allow yourself to be distracted. If something else arises which really does need your immediate attention say 'Excuse me a minute', and deal with it.

▶ Learn to cope with waffle. Continue to concentrate, searching for what is important amongst the padding. Avoid the temptation to 'switch off', you are sure to miss something important!

▶ Be sensitive as to how the speaker is feeling. If he or she is making a complaint be sympathetic (without acknowledging responsibility for the moment), remembering that the customer/client feels unhappy about the matter.

▶ Keep cool, even if the speaker is getting emotional.

▶ Ignore errors in the way the speaker says things – it is the content that matters.

▶ Take advantage of the fact that thought is faster than speech. This means that giving the matter complete concentration still allows time to analyse what is being said.

▶ Avoid thinking forward to what you are going to say since this will divert your attention. If you are listening efficiently you will have no difficulty in responding appropriately.

▶ Summarise what has been said before responding, if it is helpful in ensuring that you have understood the speaker's meaning.

Competence Builder 7 *(Elements 10.1, 10.2, 11.1, 11.2, 12.2, 14.1, 14.2, 15.1, 15.2, 19.1 and throughout)*

a) Some people who are otherwise good communicators are deficient as listeners in some way. Critically analyse your own performance as a listener. Make positive efforts to improve in the ways suggested above.

b) Discuss with your colleagues or a group of fellow students, the types of difficult customers/clients that might be met and how they can be dealt with effectively.

c) Check your knowledge of your organisation's policy and procedures for handling complaints, and keep a note for reference.

Eye Contact and Facial Expressions

▶ Establish eye contact. Looking a person in the eye encourages trust and shows interest. Conversely, looking out of the window or steadfastly elsewhere indicates lack of interest.

▶ Polish your recognition of facial cues. When you are talking to someone you can detect how they are responding by watching their faces. The expression in the eyes, position of the eyebrows, movements of the lips, wrinkling of the forehead, all indicate whether a person is listening, agrees or disagrees, is bored or interested, understands or is puzzled. You can train yourself to observe and interpret these facial signals with increasing accuracy. However, some people become very good at deceiving with their facial expressions or adopt a 'poker face', so watch out for this.

▶ Polish your own facial skills. You may find a need to cover up your own feelings at times. After all it is not prudent to reveal boredom, anxiety or what you really feel about people!

Competence Builder 8
(Elements 10.1, 10.2, 11.1, 11.2, 15.1, 15.2, and throughout)

a) Observe people when they are having conversations with others and notice what their facial expressions convey.

b) When watching television by yourself, try turning the sound down and check the extent to which you can still follow the action.

c) Stand in front of a mirror and imagine conversations with people who you have well-defined feelings about, for example individuals that you clearly like or dislike. Notice the differences in your facial expressions. How well do you think you can control these?

In order to maintain your professional relationships, you must know your organisations's specified policies and procedures for promoting and ensuring customer/client trust, goodwill and satisfaction. Constantly put these into practice, in a prompt and willing manner. If you cannot avoid delay, or the non-availability of people, goods or services, you should always explain this politely and clearly.

Competence Builder 9
(Elements 10.2, 11.1, 11.2, 12.2, 14.1, 14.2, 14.3, 15.1, 15.2)

a) In real situations or realistic simulations, and over a period of time, deal with enquiries from customers, both known and unknown. Keep a log detailing all aspects of their enquiries, and the action you took, for a minimum of 20 customers/clients.

b) Make notes which could be used to show your assessor that you understand:
   i) why essential information should be passed on promptly and accurately; and
   ii) the reasons and procedures for reporting difficulties and irregularities in your professional relationships with other members of staff, and with customers and clients.

Providing Information to Customers/Clients

As stated in Unit 1, meeting customers/clients of your organisation imposes certain obligations upon you. The obligations considered in Unit 1 and also in Unit 7, are those particular to the image you present by your appearance and manner. A further obligation is that you should be familiar with your organisation's products/services. This will enable you to respond authoritatively to specific customer/client requests for information, and when the occasion requires, identify customer/client needs prior to informing them about the relevant products/services available.

Competence Builder 1   (Elements 11.1, 11.2)

a) Make notes, for your own reference, of the general factual details of the products/services offered by your organisation.

b) Check that you have detailed knowledge of your organisation's products/services which are appropriate to the duties you might be required to carry out. If this knowledge is deficient in any way, correct this by obtaining additional information from your boss or tutor.

RESPONDING TO SPECIFIC CUSTOMER/CLIENT REQUESTS FOR INFORMATION

As in all customer/client contacts your approach should be friendly and helpful, and you should deal with the enquiries promptly and politely (see also Units 1 and 7). In some cases, the customer/client requests that the matter they are raising be dealt with confidentially, and this you must respect, ensuring that the conversation is private.

Depending upon the business in which your organisation is engaged, you will have to establish the customer's/client's eligibility to receive the information requested. This will have to be identified (using tactful questioning as required), checked and recorded according to the organisation's standard procedures. Should you find at this preliminary stage that the circumstances are outside your knowledge or responsibilities, or are not covered by your organisation's regulations, then you must refer the matter promptly to the appropriate person in higher authority.

Competence Builder 2   *(Elements 11.1, 11.2, 12.2)*

a) Find out what facilities are available in your organisation for the conduct, if required, of private interviews.

b) What criteria must be satisfied before information regarding your organisation's products/services can be passed on? Are there rules regarding the identification, verification and recording of a customer/client's eligibility to receive this information? If so, obtain or make a copy for reference.

c) Are you absolutely clear as to the limits of your responsibilities? If not, then establish these with your boss and find out to whom you should refer requests for information which go beyond these limits.

INFORMING CUSTOMERS/CLIENTS ABOUT AVAILABLE PRODUCTS AND SERVICES

The key to giving customers/clients appropriate information about products and services lies in finding out exactly what they really need. In doing so, it is important to remember that it is not necessarily what they mention in the first instance.

After listening carefully, asking questions as required and successfully establishing what is actually wanted, the next crucial step is to match the result with what your organisation can offer. It is only then that you reach the information-giving stage. This should include a clear and accurate statement of the advantages and benefits of the appropriate products/services. The match between them and the customer/client-identified needs should be pointed out, in order to emphasise that these will be met or, if the match is not exact, the extent to which they will be met. There must be no doubt in the customer's/client's mind what to expect, otherwise you could get a future complaint.

In order to obtain the required information, you may have to access paperbase and computerised information sources, so you must be competent in doing this (see Units 3, 4 and 5). You should also know your way around available written materials and be able to extract the precise information required. In carrying out this work, you must ensure that the information is accessed and made available within the period of time that it can be most effectively used. Should any relevant information not be available, then this must be explained to the customer/client and alternative arrangements made for passing on the information, when it becomes available. Any information and/or advice required which is outside of your responsibilities should be referred promptly to the appropriate person to deal with.

When passing on information in the form of written material, for example brochures, you may find that these are in short supply. Note this, and as soon as possible ensure that the material is reordered in accordance with the laid-down procedure.

Competence Builder 3   *(Elements 11.2, 12.1, 12.2, 13.1, 13.2, 13.3, 21.4 and throughout)*

a) Critically assess your competence in accessing paperbase and computerised sources of information, and negotiate with your boss or tutor an action plan for remedying any shortcomings.

b) If you do not already know then find out the procedures for the reordering of any written material available for customers/clients and keep a note of this for future reference.

c) It may be appropriate to your job role for you to be familiar with the Financial Services Act. If so, take action to familiarise yourself with the relevant aspects and keep notes on these in your file.

Communicating Effectively

The aspects of your work covered in this Unit bring into play a number of communicating skills, oral and written, the ability to recognise and respond to non-verbal communication signals, and the ability to interpret correctly oral and written information (see Units 1 and 3).

The Interview

Calling a meeting or telephone conversation with a customer/client an interview might, in some circumstances, sound rather formal. You will find, however, that whether the occasion is formal or informal, it helps to adopt interviewing techniques. The following, in particular, are useful points:

▶ Ensure privacy, if this has been requested or appears desirable.

▶ Adapt your manner to the circumstances. As well as dealing with people making straightforward enquiries you may have to cope with others who are difficult, aggressive or distressed. Remember that they feel justified in behaving in this manner, even though they may be mistaken in this attitude. You might also have to pick out the essence of the matter from a jumbled expression of feelings.

▶ Establish the customer's/client's needs. Ask tactful questions. The customer/client might not be really clear about what he or she wants and will be helped in establishing what is required by explaining the situation to you.

▶ Keep control of the situation. Do not allow the other person to digress too much.

▶ Maintain alertness, do not let your attention be diverted.

▶ Listen intently and intelligently.

▶ Be flexible, adjusting your approach as appears necessary.

▶ Do not allow yourself to become irritated.

▶ Do not allow yourself to become personally involved, be aware of any prejudice and bias on your part.

▶ Do not obviously rush the interview, but keep control of the time.

▶ Do not be influenced by the customer's/client's job title; being neither subordinate nor superior.

▶ Do not answer hastily. Speaking first and thinking afterwards is a mistake.

▶ Before offering information or undertaking research for it, check that you have correctly established the customer's/client's needs by restating what these are to the person concerned.

Competence Builder 4
(Elements 10.1, 10.2, 11.1, 11.2, 12.2, 15.1, 15.2, 19.1, 19.2, and throughout)

a) Critically assess your conversational skills (see pages 5–9). Agree with your boss or tutor an action plan for correcting any shortcomings.

b) Find out whether you will be required to make calculations as part of any information you might have to pass on regarding your organisation's products or services. If so, critically assess your ability to carry these out successfully. If you do not feel competent, ask to be shown how to make calculations of the type which might be required.

c) i) If you are in work, ask colleagues to suggest some examples of difficult situations with customers/clients in which you could find yourself. Discuss with them ways in which these situations could be resolved.

   ii) If you are in training or at college, draw up with the help of your fellow trainees or students, a list of suggested difficult customer/client meetings. Roleplay these and discuss different ways of coping with the situations.

d) Discuss with colleagues, or a group of fellow trainees or students:

   ▶ Why interviews should ensure confidentiality, and when privacy would be desirable.

   ▶ Why records of interviews should be complete and accurate.

Interview Reports

Following the interview, you may be required to write for your boss, a colleague or as a filed record, a report summarising what transpired in the interview.

What you have in effect to produce is a miniaturised version of what took place, but stating only the important parts. You must ensure that all the reader needs to know is contained in the report, but your competence in this task will be reflected as much by what you leave out as by what you include.

In drafting the report, the following points should be borne in mind:

▶ You must not let your own opinions colour your statements.

▶ You must not add personal comments.

▶ You must not alter anything that took place.

▶ You must not add other information.

It is usually safest to stick to the order of the events being summarised and, if you can do so conveniently, you will find it helpful to make brief notes during the interview.

The report should be laid out so that it is easy for the reader to grasp the content quickly, but you will have to follow your organisation's recommendations in deciding whether to present the report within a memo or as a separate document with a covering memo. Whichever method is adopted, you should state when the interview took place, with whom, where, and the reason for it. You then state the facts, followed by what was agreed, the action to be taken, etc. The date and your name should appear in a prominent place.

When making a report of an interview you may feel that it would be helpful or appropriate to ignore one of the earlier points mentioned, such as interjecting your own opinions. If so, then this should be in the form of a separate memo, thus ensuring that it is not seen as part of the interview.

Competence Builder 5

(Elements 11.1, 11.2)

In a real situation or realistic simulation:

a) Respond to a minimum of ten customers'/clients' specific requests for information on products/services offered by your organisation. Follow the guidelines given in this Unit. On at least two occasions you should be required to deal with people who are distressed. Produce records of the interviews, some of which should be summary reports.

b) Inform a minimum of ten customers/clients about the appropriate products/ services your organisation can offer, after establishing which ones are relevant to the person making the enquiry. You should be required to deal with a variety of requested information, some from people who are difficult or aggressive. Support your oral work by either written or computerised logged records showing how the enquiries were dealt with.

Researching and Presenting Information

You will find that your reputation as a competent clerical worker will be enhanced if you know where to find information when it is needed and you can demonstrate your ability to assess its accuracy and reliability.

In most cases, you will not be expected to carry details in your head, but you must know where they can be obtained. It is this ability to tap into appropriate reference sources which is so valuable and is an essential part of the competence you are seeking.

SOURCES OF INFORMATION

The first place to search for information should always be amongst the records in your organisation which are in everyday use or to which you have easy access. This could include records stored in folders, on cards and lists, on microfilm and on computer files. These immediate sources of reference should yield information on regularly referred to matters, such as those to do with customers and suppliers.

You might encounter difficulty in gaining access to filing systems which are restricted and may need to consult a colleague who is permitted access. You should, in any event, expect to use your colleagues as reference sources. In addition to being easily available they may also be familiar with the matter you are researching or have records which can be referred to.

Competence Builder 1   *(Elements 11.1, 11.2, 12.2, 15.1, 19.1, 19.2)*

a) List the information systems in your organisation to which you have

   i) free access; and
   ii) access via a colleague.

b) State, next to the name of each system, the main areas of information you would expect to obtain from each one.

c) If you are authorised to obtain information from any sources in your organisation with which you are not yet familiar, for example, microfiche or computer files, ask for instruction on accessing these and take any opportunities to practise.

Catalogues and Price Lists

These use a classified grouping system, i.e. items which seem to belong together are grouped together, rather than being listed, for example, in alphabetical order. Within each grouping, alphabetical order might be applied, but criteria such as size, quantity or price are more common. Catalogues include descriptions of the products whereas price lists only list items and their prices. Because prices change constantly catalogues are often printed without prices and an up-to-date price list is inserted before being sent out to customers/clients.

Computer Databank Services

These are other sources to which you might be able to refer, from within your own organisation. Upon accessing a computer databank service, information is shown on the screen of a television receiver or similar equipment. The service might be a private one, such as a bank's database of customer accounts or one available to the public, such as those operated by British Telecom and the television companies, i.e. *Ceefax* and *Oracle*. Stockmarket reports, foreign exchange news, news headlines, air services and other travel information (including weather maps), are all examples of the type of information available, and the range is increasing.

Reference Books

Your organisation probably has some standard reference books available for regular use by staff. If you want information which does not appear in these, but which is likely to be found in a reference book, then this might be available at your local library. If necessary, ask a librarian for assistance. Knowing exactly where to look for information is a skill which takes time to acquire and problems can arise in using an index and cross-references. You may prevent some difficulties, when consulting a reference book, if you always check to see if there is a section stating how that particular book should be used.

Competence Builder 2

(Elements 12.2, 14.1, 14.3, 15.1, 16.1, 17.1, 18.1, 19.1, 19.2)

a) Make a list of the reference books available in your organisation to which you might need to refer. State where they are located and add a broad statement regarding their contents.

b) Spend some time browsing in your local library reference section, in order to gain a general picture of the range of books available there. Make reference notes of any relevant to your work.

c) Negotiate with the librarian a convenient time when you can be advised of some of the difficulties which may be encountered when using a reference book index. Discussing these will help you to begin to acquire a strategy for coping with them.

Trade Journals

These relate to a particular trade or profession, and are usually published weekly or monthly. They report on the latest developments and give news of particular interest to a trade or profession. Most libraries carry a range of trade journals with current issues on display. In some cases back copies are kept for reference and are available upon request. Trade journals and periodicals are often the best source of reference when the most up-to-date information is required, but this may take some finding. Examples of reference books which can be used to find the titles of appropriate trade journals and periodicals are *Willing's Press Guide* and *Benn's Media Directory*.

Competence Builder 3 *(Elements 12.2, 19.1, 19.2, 21.4)*

a) List the categories of trade journals kept in your local library.

b) Find out the extent of the library and information services available in your local telephone area. Keep a copy of these sources of information, listed in alphabetical order.

UK Government Publications

These are available mainly through Her Majesty's Stationery Office (HMSO), which has branches or agencies in large towns and cities. HMSO Publications are also available by post. These publications include books and documents on parliamentary business, such as *Hansard*, the official report of Parliamentary proceedings. A variety of matters, such as census data and other digests of statistics, and advice to businesses, are dealt with in other publications. A useful, free, annual booklet *Government Statistics: A Brief Guide to Resources*, gives advice on how to find and use government statistics. This is available from the Central Statistical Office (CSO).

Other Information Agencies

If the information you require cannot be found within your own organisation or from easily accessible printed sources, then contacting an outside body, such as the local Chamber of Commerce, may yield results. Your organisation might even be a member of certain trade bodies or organisations from which you can seek help, but remember that often you will be asking for information to be given on a voluntary basis.

When seeking such voluntary information you should always remember that it is causing work for other people. You cannot take it for granted that they are prepared to do work for you or indeed are willing to pass on any information that you request. You should, therefore, indicate why you are making the enquiry and the importance of it. Be appreciative of the help given and similarly be prepared to give help to those requiring information from you.

Even with a great deal of searching and seeking advice there will be occasions when you are unable to find the exact information. There will also be occasions where there is a choice of reference material. You should, therefore, be prepared to suggest alternatives when you cannot meet the requirements exactly, and offer the options where these exist.

If your research is to be carried out thoroughly you must be familiar with, and competent in using, the available communication services, for example, telephone, telex and facsimile (fax) services (see Unit 6).

Competence Builder 4   *(Elements 12.2, 14.1, 14.3, 15.1, 19.1, 19.2)*

a) Draw up for reference, a list of the sources of information, appropriate to your work, to which you might need to refer.

b) Ask your boss or tutor for opportunities to practise identifying sources and abstracting information to meet specific requests, and so build up your competence in doing these tasks.

READING COMPETENTLY

Your reading skills must be well-developed, in order to make full use of written materials as reference sources. To be competent in researching information you must be able to not only read words, but understand what the author intends to convey, i.e. the sense of the text.

This does not mean that you have to read laboriously and consider carefully every single word of every piece of written material you are working on. There are different ways of reading and the way you choose should be the one most appropriate to the task.

Reading Depth

Skim reading is appropriate when all that is written is not relevant to your task and you have to search for the relevant parts. An example of this would be when you skip through a reference book in order to find a specific entry. You would of course check the index first.

Skim reading would obviously not be appropriate when the relevant entry is found, if information has to be abstracted from it. What we think of as 'normal' reading would be appropriate in this case.

If the entry deals with a complex issue and it is difficult to understand points, then in-depth reading would be required. Specific meanings of words would be important and any unfamiliar ones would have to be checked in a dictionary. This type of reading is slower, but necessary if the information gathered is to be accurate. It also has valuable bonuses in that you gain greater familiarity with the meaning of words, your reading speed improves as your vocabulary increases and you need to look up fewer words in the dictionary, and you will become better at communicating, both as a sender and as a receiver.

Reading for Facts

Recognising the difference between facts and opinions is another aspect of reading competently. This becomes obvious when researching in newspapers and magazines. A danger to be aware of here is that it is easy to accept as fact opinions which you agree with and dismiss as opinions the statements which you do not agree with!

Information is sometimes presented in such a way that it is ambiguous and may even be deliberately misleading. You must therefore question anything unclear, and seek confirmation or rejection of it from another source if you are still not certain. This ensures that the information you finally obtain is correct.

Competence Builder 5 *(Elements 12.2)*

Take a mixed selection of magazine and newspaper items. Underline the facts and circle the opinions. Was it easy to distinguish between them?

Reading Quickly

You can only take in the number of words you see at one time and so reading speed is conditioned by eye span. This span, which differs from one person to another, can be increased with practice. Since research time is reduced by being able to read quickly, it is obviously worthwhile practising techniques in order to improve. Here are a few simple ones:

▶ Practise reading credits at the end of a television programme. These frequently move very fast and have to be read individually; they cannot be deduced, as is the case with continuous prose.

▶ When reading a newspaper or magazine item, pick out a key word then quickly count the number of times that word appears. Check slowly a second time to find out what percentage of the total was originally 'seen'. Practise on other items, trying to improve your percentage success rate.

▶ Practise reading car registration numbers when travelling; this will speed up number recognition.

Competence Builder 6   *(Elements 11.2, 12.2, 15.1, 19.1, 19.2 and throughout)*

Practise the suggested techniques for improving reading speed. Test your reading speed before you start. Devise a simple chart for recording your progress.

PRESENTING INFORMATION

On many occasions when you are asked for information, the way in which you should present this will be specified or will be obvious, for example, orally, in writing, graphically or a combination of these. In some instances the choice will be left to you. If this is so, then you must present the information in the most appropriate manner. In making a choice, bear in mind the following case for incorporating graphics in your presentation.

▶ Spoken words have the advantage of being immediate, but what the words convey and the order in which they are given, is decided by the speaker. The listener has little control over what to deal with and when, until the speaker has finished.

▶ Written material gives the reader more control over the order in which matters are dealt with because it can be skimmed before reading in depth. Even so the decision what to deal with and when is not as easy with words as it is with graphics, where you can glance at the information as a whole.

▶ Words alone, spoken or written, are limited when you are trying to describe complicated or unusual movements, items (such as pieces of equipment), or are trying to show where something is placed in relation to something else (such as when giving directions).

▶ Words combined with a lot of numbers convey little to the listener or the reader. Diagrams, tables, graphs and charts convey this type of information much more effectively.

Diagrams

A diagram is made up of outlines and does not attempt to show actual appearances. In the type of diagram which is often called a plan, it is usual to draw to scale with the plan representing the whole area. An example could be a room, with a plan being used to decide where furniture will be best placed. Cut-out shapes represent the furniture and these are moved around the plan in order to decide the optimum arrangement. Thus, all the information needed is available from the beginning and anyone setting about the task of creating a satisfactory room arrangement can decide where to begin.

Plans are also drawn of larger areas, for example, town street plans, and may or may not be to scale (see Figure 3.1). If you are giving someone directions on how to reach a certain location, you may draw a sketch map, which is a type of diagram.

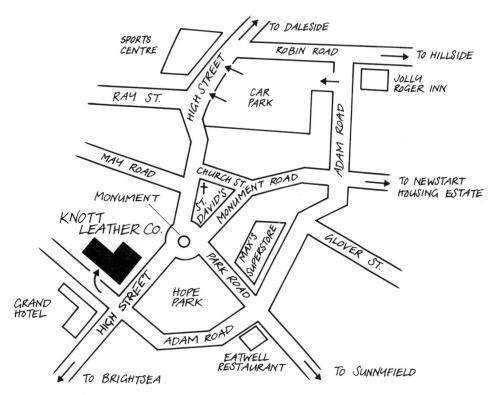

Figure 3.1 Plan of Kent town showing location of Knott Leather Company (not drawn to scale)

This is not usually drawn to scale. A good example of a plan which is not drawn to scale is that of the London Underground system. This shows all the essential details, such as order of stations, without showing distances to scale.

Diagrams are used for many purposes, such as to show how items of equipment work and how things are assembled. Whether precisely or roughly drawn, they are convenient to use if they convey the information more clearly than words alone.

Tables

A table (basically labelled columns) can be useful when you need to communicate information that includes a large quantity of complicated numbers. In designing tables so that they convey information clearly, apply the following:

▶ Choose column headings which are unambiguous and, for ease of reading and design, short.

▶ State what the numbers represent, for example £ or %, immediately under the column heading.

▶ Space out the table so that numbers in adjoining columns do not appear to merge, yet are not so far apart that they are difficult to compare.

▶ Within each column, always place the tens, hundreds, decimal points, etc., exactly under each other.

▶ Draw up a key for any abbreviations used and ensure that this is prominently displayed.

▶ Write a caption to the table which states clearly and concisely what the table represents and over which period the data refers to.

	Sales in categories and total sale for one year				
	1986 (£000s)	1987 (£000s)	1988 (£000s)	1989 (£000s)	1990 (£000s)
Men's shoes	82.00	76.00	70.00	66.25	66.00
Women's shoes	95.00	95.00	107.50	132.50	110.00
Children's shoes	68.00	66.50	85.00	103.75	97.50
Travel/Handbags	108.00	95.00	109.00	95.00	115.00
Miscellaneous	41.00	47.50	77.00	132.50	140.00
Total sales	394.00	380.00	448.50	530.00	528.50

Comparison of one category over several years

Figure 3.2 Comparison of sales of Knott Leather Company, 1986–90

Figure 3.2 shows a table comparing sales over the period 1986–90 for the Knott Leather Company.

You need to consider carefully what it is you want to depict when deciding upon the form of your graphic. Figure 3.2 can be used for two purposes. If the table is read vertically it shows the sales in categories and the total sales for each year; if it is read horizontally it shows how the sales in each of the categories differed in the years given. If the graphic you choose can present two different pictures, you need to ask yourself if you should choose another type which would better illustrate what you really intend and so avoid possible confusion.

Graphs

Line graphs are long-established and well-known. They are very good for portraying trends and fluctuations over a period of time, and thus can be used advantageously to draw attention to features requiring investigation and explanation.

Competence Builder 7 (Element 12.2)

Check your competence in constructing line graphs by either:

▶ drawing up a graph which is required by your boss; or

▶ drawing up a graph to compare the sales of the Knott Leather Company for the period 1986–90 for men's, women's and children's shoes.

Charts

Charts are very good for making comparisons because differences show up sharply, but getting people to make the desired comparison depends upon the type of chart chosen.

Pie Charts

Taking the data given in Figure 3.2, a pie chart would be the most effective choice if you wanted to show the relative size of the sales of each category of goods as a proportion of total sales, for one particular year. The whole circle represents the total sales in one year and this is divided into segments which then represent the sales for each category. The relative sizes of the segments present a clear and easy-to-judge, at-a-glance picture, but if you also include the percentage amounts of sales in each segment, the information is more precise. When deciding to use this form of chart you must bear in mind the number of items to be included or group several related items, since it is generally best to restrict pie chart segments to four or five. Another factor in deciding to use this type of chart is the complexity of the data. From a practical point of view, the choice of a pie chart should be restricted to where figures are simple, otherwise it becomes difficult to construct.

Competence Builder 8 (Element 12.2)

Check your competence in drawing pie charts by either:

▶ drawing a pie chart required by your boss; or

▶ drawing a pie chart using the 1987 sales figures of the Knott Leather Company. Include the percentage figure in each segment.

Bar Charts

In their more usual form, these are a variation of the line graph. Statistics on bar charts are shown not as points on a scale but as bars or oblongs proportional to the figures. The bars can be drawn horizontally or vertically against a scale, so that it can be seen what the actual numbers are that the bars represent. Differences show up clearly so bar charts are particularly good for making comparisons. One disadvantage of using a bar chart is that the bars take up a lot of space, so the chart has to be confined to a short time sequence.

Pictograms are a form of bar chart. The bars are replaced by rows of little pictures of what the chart is about, for example, little houses on a chart showing the number of houses built each month over a period of months (see Figure 3.3). These are often used in magazines and advertising to get a message across to the general public more pictorially.

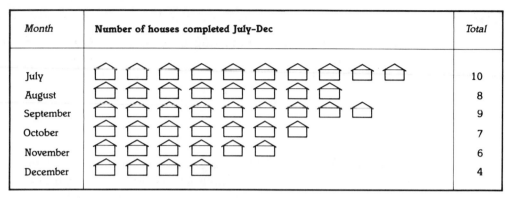

Figure 3.3 Pictogram showing number of houses completed over a period of six months on Newstart Housing Estate, Kent town

Competence Builder 9
(Element 12.2)

Check your competence in drawing up bar charts by either:

▶ drawing a bar chart required by your boss; or

▶ drawing up a bar chart to compare the 1987 and 1989 Knott Leather Company's sales of men's, women's and children's shoes.

Designing Graphics

Squared graph paper will help you to draw charts and graphs neatly and accurately. Neatness is very important so do take care when joining the dots or small crosses on line graphs. Provide a key for any symbols that you use.

Draw to as large a scale as the paper will allow and state what this scale represents. The divisions on a scale normally represent units of multiples of five or ten. A useful plotting rule is to always plot the factor which does not change (for example, time) along the horizontal axis and the factor which does change (for example, quantity) along the vertical axis.

In order to avoid distorted impressions the same scale must be retained when two or more bar charts or line graphs are drawn for comparison. For the same reason bar charts should, wherever possible, start from zero on the vertical axis.

Remember that the reason for using graphics is to replace or clarify written information. To be of real value a graphic must make an impact; something simple will usually achieve this better than something complicated. Adding colour or shading heightens the impact, provided this is not overdone.

When a lot of information has to be communicated, it is important to consider what is best written and what is best illustrated. Too many illustrations interrupt the flow of the narrative and become a distraction. One way of avoiding this is to present them as an appendix. In the appendix they should appear in the same order as they would in the text, be given appropriate titles and be numbered. They should be referred to by these numbers in the text.

Competence Builder 10
(Elements 12.2, 13.1, 13.2, 13.3)

Much of the work of converting data to graphics can now be achieved quickly and accurately using computers. If you are in a position to do so negotiate opportunities to practise producing graphics of the type mentioned in this Unit on a computer.

Composition of Notes, Memos and Letters

In many cases, you will be presenting in written form the information you have gathered. This might be as a note, a memo or a letter. Whichever method you use you have to plan and organise your material, and use words effectively with correct grammar, spelling and punctuation.

Competence Builder 11
(Elements 10.2, 12.2, 14.3, 16.1, 17.1, 18.1 and throughout)

If you have difficulty with the mechanics of language (grammar, spelling and punctuation) then you must make arrangements to improve, otherwise your competence will always be marred. Critically assess your ability to write correctly. If you have any problems discuss with your boss or tutor ways in which you can be helped to make improvements, such as attending classes, working through an open learning text or being given more opportunities for practising written language skills.

Planning and Organising

For ease of reading and understanding, a written communication needs to be presented in chunks. These chunks take the form of paragraphs or sections. Each chunk should be complete in itself, and the parts of the chunks, for example, the sentences should all have something in common.

These chunks have then to be presented in a logical order. This generally commences with some form of introduction so that the reader has some indication of what is to follow. It is not necessary for this to be wordy and quite often a heading serves as a sufficient introduction. The main body then follows. The order this takes is sometimes predetermined in that certain things must be mentioned first otherwise what follows will not be understood. If the order is not obvious then a pattern should be adopted following certain rules such as:

▶ Chronological order – an obvious choice for describing events since these are given in the order in which they took place.

▶ Descending order of importance – a common method for business communications since the important points are stated first with the less important ones following.

▶ Ascending order of importance – useful for arguing a cause, since this is built up with the strongest points left to the end, for finally proving the case.

▶ From the known to the unknown – good for describing how a piece of equipment works. You start with what the reader knows already and add the new information in stages, thus gradually building up the necessary knowledge.

▶ From the simple to the complex – you state the simplest points first, working up to the more difficult, in the anticipation that the readers will, in this way, build up their understanding.

A conclusion should be used to end most written communication. If the matter is complex this can summarise what has gone before, but in many cases it will simply be to round off the communication.

One further aspect in organising your writing is the use of headings and subheadings. These help to break up the material and allow the reader to note the content at a glance. It also helps the reader to pick out immediately anything of particular interest. Headings and subheadings are especially helpful when it is necessary for a document to be discussed or referred to in a reply.

Another aid to reference is the use of numbers and letters for the various sections and subsections. Decimals are also used, for example, 1.1, 1.2, and so on. You should follow the systems which have been employed previously if you are working on something already established. You should also know your organisation's preferred methods.

Competence Builder 12   *(Elements 10.2, 11.1, 12.2, 16.1, 17.1, 18.1 and throughout)*

Check with your boss or tutor your knowledge and use of notes, memos and letters. Do you always use these appropriately and lay them out correctly? Seek to correct any deficiencies by asking for work which will give you practice in using these methods as a means of supplying information.

Summarising

You will most likely produce a summary at some time or another as a means of passing on information. Summary writing is a skill which depends on reading with understanding, since it is difficult to write an accurate summary unless you have fully understood the original material.

Your summary should be concise and divided into easily digested sections. In writing, it is usually safest to follow the order of the material being summarised. Use note form headings, number and letter references, and state the source(s), where appropriate. Add a title, the date and your name, so that further information can be obtained if necessary.

In writing summaries remember that you are concerned solely with the writer's ideas and must not, therefore:

▶ let your own ideas or opinions colour the summary;

▶ add personal comments;

▶ discuss the opinions given;

▶ add other information;

▶ alter the balance of any arguments presented. (Generalisations are acceptable provided you quote important details in full.)

A pitfall in summarising is to reduce the number of words to the extent that the points made are not clear. When you read through the draft of your summary think of the reader and consider whether or not what you have written is comprehensible when the original has not been seen.

Competence Builder 13   *(Elements 10.2, 11.2, 12.2)*

Summarise the section 'Reading Competently' and keep this for reference.

Writing Clearly

Written words appear to be more authoritative than spoken words and of course much written material is filed away as a permanent record. Perhaps it is this awareness that prompts people to write in a long-winded, formal manner, particularly in business. This is neither necessary nor desirable. Business correspondence is best written with the points made as briefly as possible, using common rather than uncommon words.

Reliability is important and can be improved if you:

▶ Think about what you have to say, and for whom it is intended, before you write anything.

▶ Jot the ideas down and then sort them into logical order.

▶ Divide up your ideas into chunks, each of which is complete in itself.

▶ Write briefly, simply and to the point.

▶ Vary your sentence length and structure.

▶ Give your writing a smooth flow and continuity. This is done by introducing phrases which carry on to the next sentence or tie back a sentence to the one which has gone before.

Avoid stock phrases, jargon and 'fashionable long windedness'. For example, do not use 'at this moment in time' but use 'now' instead.

▶ Write a rough copy first or, ideally, key it into a word processor. You can then check spellings against a dictionary, correct punctuation, cut out slang, and check that there is no ambiguity in what you have written.

Competence Builder 14

(Elements 10.2, 11.1, 11.2, 12.2)

In real situations or realistic simulations respond to requests for information. You should be required to present the information in the form of tables, diagrams, graphs, notes, memos and letters; the display format selected being suitable for the intended purpose. Should the exact information required not be available, you should be prepared to offer an alternative. Where there is a choice of material, you should offer the options. In each case you should work to a deadline.

Maintaining an Established Filing System

Offices receive large quantities of information. Some of it can be quickly disposed of, but much of it must be kept for future possible reference. If retrieval is to be swift and easy then filing must be carried out according to rules which can be understood and followed by everyone concerned. These rules apply to filing correctly and to retrieving the information.

Filing systems must keep information safely and neatly, with access to anything confidential being limited. This Unit deals primarily with the traditional, paper-based systems still widely used and, given the variety and type of information currently stored in them, apparently set to continue despite the advent of new technology. However, computerised systems are on the increase and you must aim to become competent in using them (see Competence Builder 11 in this Unit and also Unit 5).

Filing is one of the most common duties of a clerical worker and thus it may be part of your job. Unfortunately, because much of the work is routine, its importance is not always stressed, and people are ill-informed regarding the systems or become careless. You must not be guilty of this. Incorrectly filed records can be virtually lost in a filing system, and cause increased costs, delay, frustration, loss of goodwill and even loss of business. It is vital, therefore, that you are knowledgeable about the systems to which you have access. If you have filing responsibilities you must be constantly on guard to ensure that problems do not arise.

CENTRALISED AND DEPARTMENTAL FILING

Particularly in larger organisations the bulk of the filing is carried out by a central filing department. There is an argument for such a department to deal with the organisation's filing in its entirety; the opposing point of view argues that files should be under the control of the department which uses them.

When filing is centralised it is dealt with by staff who are employed specifically as filing clerks. It can be expected therefore that they will be knowledgeable about the system and operate it efficiently. Their supervisor can concentrate on setting up and maintaining effective and efficient methods for ensuring that files are always available when required. Centralisation may mean that better use can be made of available space and the purchase of elaborate equipment could prove to be cost-effective. A standardised system of filing can be established which should be more efficient because there is only one system to learn about.

Standardisation can however be a disadvantage because a system which suits the work of one department does not necessarily suit the work of another. For example, an export department might consider filing by location (geographical filing) the most useful, while the advertising department might prefer to file by subject. To overcome this problem, and that of restricting access to confidential information, a mixed system is frequently operated. Departmental filing systems run in parallel with central filing. The filing system in each department can then be the one which best suits the department's work. Files are more readily available for those who use them the most frequently, confidentiality is easier to maintain, and filing accuracy is improved because the staff handling departmental files are the most familiar with the matters dealt with in them.

A departmental filing system is usually small and sometimes nobody is actually in charge of it. It is however usually more efficient if someone is given responsibility for ensuring that the filing is done efficiently and that information is provided as and when it is required. You might find yourself in this position.

Competence Builder 1   *(Element 12.1)*

How are files kept in your organisation – centrally, departmentally or mixed? Make enquiries and find out the reasons why this arrangement is in operation.

CLASSIFICATION AND CONTROL

Correspondence is filed under the name of the organisation on whose behalf a person has written, unless it is purely personal. The order in which files are placed is based on one of the standard systems of classification: alphabetical, by subject, geographical or numerical.

Alphabetical Filing

This is a popular system which you will almost certainly find yourself using many times during your working life. Files are made out under the name of the correspondent or organisation, and these files are then arranged in strict alphabetical order. For each letter of the alphabet there is also a 'miscellaneous' file into which papers of insufficient quantity to warrant individual files are placed. These miscellaneous files are often used for separating the batches of files for each letter of the alphabet. There are other means of doing this, for example, using cards known as 'guide cards'.

The major advantage of this system is that it is simple to manage without any need to refer to an index. One disadvantage is that it is difficult to assess how much space needs to be allowed between the batches of files for each letter of the alphabet, for the addition of new files. This can result in space being wasted or time being spent in shifting files and reorganising cabinets.

A more serious disadvantage arises from the difficulty of applying a standard system of alphabetical order. There are many variations which can be introduced by people handling the files. One solution is to have only one person handling the files, but this is often not practical. The solution usually adopted is to have a set of rules which everyone using the system must strictly adhere to.

Competence Builder 2 *(Elements 12.1, 16.1, 17.1, 18.1, 21.1, 21.2)*

This is for those who have not already proved their competence in alphabetical order filing.

a) If you have yet to prove your knowledge of the standard alphabetical order filing rules find these out and make yourself a list. Check with your boss or tutor that you have included all the rules.

b) Ask for opportunities to learn thoroughly about, and use, an alphabetical order filing system if this is not currently part of your duties. If there is insufficient time for you to do this then ask if you can prove your knowledge of the alphabetical order rules by pre-sorting the filing on a number of occasions.

Subject Filing

In this system, documents are filed under subject headings rather than under the names of the correspondents or organisations. It can be extremely useful, but to use this method efficiently you must be thoroughly familiar with the organisation's business. There is an increased possibility of misfiling and of opening a new file when one already exists on that topic under a different name. For this reason, you need to have an adequately cross-referenced index.

Subject filing is useful, for example, in a purchasing office, because it is convenient to file together the price lists and catalogues from a number of suppliers under a heading indicating the type of goods supplied. There could, therefore, be files for office stationery, office equipment and office furniture. This makes it easier to find suppliers when certain goods are required and allows for rapid comparison of what each supplier has to offer.

Each major section might then be subdivided – office equipment into typewriters, telecommunications equipment, computers and so on. Cross-referencing is then needed if one supplier deals in equipment in several categories and the possibility of error is increased.

Subject filing is often used for keeping together all papers relating to a particular topic or activity, where it is the topic that is of prime importance and not the people involved. This would apply to committee and general business matters. It is usual to maintain alphabetical order within each subject grouping, but this can be varied if it makes for easier reference to files when they are required.

Geographical Filing

As the name indicates, this system requires files to be grouped in geographical order, by country, county, town and so on. The files are then placed within each geographical division, either by name or subject. Alphabetical order is maintained within each division and subdivision. Since all the files for a certain area are kept together this system is a logical and convenient one to use for departments such as sales, export and transport (see Figure 4.1).

There are disadvantages. For example:

▶ not all of an organisation's activities are carried out strictly according to geographical divisions;

▶ problems can arise if you are not sure of geographical locations and it is time-consuming to check these constantly;

▶ you might need an index which links correspondents with the geographical division in which their file can be found.

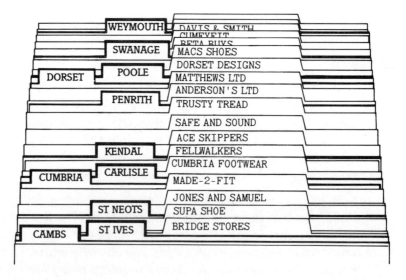

Figure 4.1 Geographical order filing

Competence Builder 3 *(Elements 12.1, 16.1, 17.1, 18.1, 21.1, 21.2)*

a) Find out what classification systems are in use in your organisation for filing. Discuss with your boss or tutor whether or not there could be an argument for using the subject or geographical systems where these are not already used. If this is not appropriate for your organisation, list some organisations which would find subject and geographical filing useful and state why.

b) If subject and geographical systems are operated in your organisation ask for an opportunity to work on them, shadow someone, i.e. sit in with someone who is working on them, or get someone to show you how they are operated.

Numerical Filing

This system is particularly convenient where new files are being opened regularly. New files are placed at the back of the existing ones, so expansion is no problem.

Consecutive numbers are allotted to correspondents. An alphabetical index is kept, showing the number of each file and, when a file is required, the index is referred to in order to obtain its number. Apart from ease of expansion there are a number of other advantages:

▶ numbered files are easier to find than alphabetical ones and are less likely to be misplaced when refiled;

▶ the file number provides a useful reference and, if this is used on letters, it eliminates the need to refer to the index;

▶ use can be made of the index for other purposes, such as creating a mailing list.

There are also disadvantages. Although a numbered file can be found more easily than an alphabetical one, you have to first obtain the number from an alphabetical index. This adds time to the process, as does the need to keep the index up-to-date. It is also easy to make an error in filing as a result of transposing numbers, i.e. reading 45 for 54. This is very common and can lead to serious misplacing of records. You must, therefore, take particular care to ensure that you do not do this.

Competence Builder 4 *(Elements 12.1, 16.1, 17.1, 18.1, 21.1, 21.2)*

Seek some way of increasing your knowledge and experience of a numerical filing system. If one is in use in your organisation ask to have the opportunity of working on it, of shadowing someone who works on it or of being shown how it operates. Discuss with someone familiar with the system why it is considered the best choice and what or if problems arise.

Chronological Filing

Papers within each file are normally placed in chronological (date) order. It is usual to place the most-recently dated item on the top and the oldest on the bottom.

Chronological order is also used for bring-forward (follow-up) systems. These cater for instances where jobs have to be done, for example, sending out notices of meetings to be held or requests for information met at a certain time, but the relevant papers are not likely to be needed in the interim period. They are, therefore, filed away, but a reminder system is set up for ensuring that the papers are 'brought forward' at the time required.

New Files

Sometimes you will need to make out a new file. This might be for a fresh correspondent or it might be that a number of papers for one correspondent have accumulated in a miscellaneous file. Also, when a file becomes too bulky you may need to start a number two file for that correspondent. In deciding to make out a new file you must abide by the rules laid down, for example, that the setting-up of a new file has to be authorised by some more senior person.

New files should be made out and labelled in a manner consistent with the rest of the filing system. If there is an index, for example, for a numerical system, enter the new file on it. When placing the new file in the system make sure that there is sufficient room for it and make any necessary adjustments.

Retention and Disposal

Particularly in paper-based systems the sheer volume of paper makes it necessary to sift the contents of the files, throwing out what is no longer required. This over-loading is obvious with paper records. Perhaps one danger of computerised filing lies in the quantity of information that can be accommodated in a small space and its ease of access. 'Weeding' the files is then not as obviously a job which needs to be kept under control.

Keeping the job under control is accomplished by an annual turnout or as an ongoing job. Particularly in a large organisation, there may be a general policy for the retention and disposal of documents. In these cases, retention periods for different types of documents are set, which allow the sifting to be carried out partly by the filing staff. Where there are no definite guidelines then the sifting is more likely to be an executive or senior job.

Documents which are not current, but which need to be kept for possible future reference, are usually moved to the archives section. They are placed in envelopes or boxes, suitably indexed and stored. This needs to be in an accessible place but not one where space is at a premium such as where current files are kept. If there are both current and archive files for a correspondent then the fact that an archive file exists must be stated somewhere prominent, for example, inside the front cover.

Competence Builder 5

(Element 12.1)

Find out and keep notes on:

a) How the decision to create a new file is made in your organisation, who makes it, and how you would carry out the task of opening the file.

b) Your organisation's retention policy or, if a policy does not exist, how the task of weeding the files is dealt with.

c) The legal constraints which apply in your organisation on the storage and retention of records.

d) The rules of your organisation which determine when a number two and/or an archive file is created.

Booking-out Systems

When someone wants a file it is irritating, time-wasting and costly if it is missing. In order to avoid this, a system that ensures that the file can be traced without delay is needed.

One such system uses 'absent folders', preferably of a different colour from the normal file folders, to make the absent folders easily noticed. One of these is inserted in place of the file being removed. Into it is slipped a form showing the name or number of the removed file, and who currently has it. If you also add the date the file is borrowed it encourages people to return files as soon as possible.

The absent folder can be used for placing papers in whilst the actual file is out. Although convenient for this purpose, it can cause problems because the person using the file is without the most up-to-date papers. This might affect work being done or decisions which have to be made. A safer practice to follow is to take additional papers as they come in to the person who has the file so that it is as up-to-date as possible. You should request that these papers be added, in the correct order, into the file; alternatively, do this yourself if it is convenient.

A similar system uses a card for each absent file on which is recorded who has the file. The card is placed where the file would normally be. Another alternative is to record file movements in a register. The advantage of this is that it can be easily seen which files are out and for how long. Chasing-up files and requesting their prompt return then becomes easier.

Competence Builder 6

(Element 12.1)

What system operates in your organisation for recording the whereabouts of borrowed files? Make a copy for yourself of these instructions either typed or, if convenient, a photocopy.

Safety and Confidentiality

Careless use of filing equipment creates safety hazards. You must make sure that you are aware of the dangers, are observant, and take care to avoid injury to yourself and others.

Some matters with which your organisation deals will be confidential. The records regarding these should be placed in files which are clearly marked 'confidential'. The files should be locked away when not in use. When they are in use they must never be left open or in any place where an unauthorised person could read the contents.

The general files should be in cabinets which can be locked at night. You should never issue a file to someone who does not normally have access to them without first consulting a more senior person.

Since use can be made of information not obviously confidential, it is usually safest to shred documents thrown out as a result of weeding files or discarded for any other reason.

Competence Builder 7   (Element 12.1)

a) Make a list of the safety hazards specifically associated with filing. Be observant and note the points made in this Unit.

b) Find out which files are confidential in your organisation and if there is a laid-down policy regarding the confidentiality of files.

c) Check, and keep a note or photocopy of your organisation's rules for the disposal of unwanted records.

General Rules

There are general rules which apply to filing regardless of the systems adopted. You will find that your actual filing time will be reduced and be more efficient if you follow these rules and are systematic in your work.

▶ File daily – particularly if other people are also using the files. A wrong decision could be made because the most up-to-date papers were sitting in the 'To be filed' tray. Filing at the same time each day helps to instil the habit and the job is done as a matter of course.

▶ Follow your organisation's system for checking that all papers have been cleared for filing. An example of such a system is the requirement that papers ready for filing are initialled or similarly marked to indicate this.

▶ If items to be filed are a mixture of documents, for example, papers, folders and catalogues, then separate them into these categories first.

▶ Sort into categories according to the filing system – this will save a lot of walking about and unnecessary use of filing equipment.

▶ Circle, or underline in red, the name under which the papers are to be filed. This helps to avoid error and speeds up the filing. Marking-up can however become automatic and you should take care that mistakes do not occur as a result of your not giving sufficient attention to the job.

▶ Sort papers into batches in the order in which they will be filed. Use any equipment provided, i.e. a sorter, to help you to speed up this work.

▶ Staple related papers together. Do not file paper clips, they add bulk and other papers get caught in them. Remove pins, they can cause injury.

Now file each batch of papers taking care over the following:

▶ Check that every paper is placed in the correct file. Misfiled papers can cause untold trouble and loss to your organisation.

▶ Check that every paper is placed in the correct order in the file; chronologically with the most recent document on the top.

▶ Place papers neatly and squarely in the folders. It is easier to do so if the files are taken out rather than attempting to slide papers into them.

▶ Where required to do so, make out new files, labelling them neatly and clearly.

▶ If authorised to do so, split bulky files into two and clearly label them with the name adding 'File 1 (from date to date)', 'File 2 (from date–current)'.

▶ Thin files out regularly. Even if you are not required to do so personally you might have to take some action regarding this and should know your organisation's policy.

▶ Check miscellaneous files every time anything is filed in them. If there are several letters to, or from, one correspondent (say five or six papers), and contact seems likely to continue, it is usual to make out a separate file.

▶ Cross-reference wherever there is a possibility that papers might be looked for in more than one place. A convenient way of doing this is to decide under which of the two names the papers will be filed, then make out a file for the alternative name. This extra file is left empty, apart from a note placed on or in it referring the seeker to the file which does contain the papers.

▶ Renew folders when they become worn or at least make a note to do so when time permits.

▶ When papers are required from the filing system remove the whole file concerned otherwise some other person may use the file not realising that it is incomplete. Use a booking-out system.

Competence Builder 8

(Element 12.1)

Write or type-up your own version of these rules for reference. Extract only the key point from each rule and include only those appropriate to your job circumstances.

Bring-forward Systems

These are sometimes known as 'tickler' files because they tickle the memory at an appropriate time. There are different ways of setting them up but the aim is that matters are dealt with at the appropriate time and are not forgotten. You will find a follow-up system useful:

▶ If someone has been written to with a query. Then it is wise to keep a note in order to check that an answer is received.

▶ If documents are going to be needed in the future for a meeting or some such purpose. Then there needs to be some method of ensuring that they are brought forward at that time.

A diary, a personal organiser, such as a *Filofax*, or a computerised diary planner, can be used for personal reminders. If the reminders have to serve a number of people or papers have to be kept in the follow-up system, then the following system is likely to prove satisfactory.

A follow-up system is put together using a concertina file, wallet folders or the file folders used for the rest of the filing system. The concertina file sections or folders are labelled January to December. Behind the folder for the current month there should be 31 divider cards or sheets of stiff paper labelled 1 to 31 for each day of the month (see Figure 4.2).

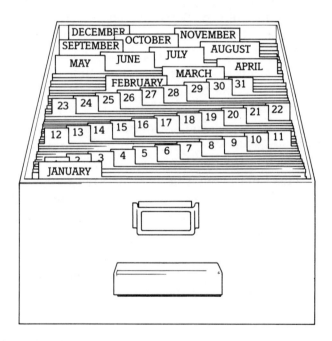

Figure 4.2 Bring-forward system

Some way of 'tickling' the memory has then to be set up. A form is one means. On this is stated the name of the file, some identification of the particular documents wanted, the date they are required and the name of the person making the request. These are placed in the folders for the months on which a follow-up is required.

An alternative is to take a copy of the document to be followed-up (or the first page of a batch) and write on it the follow-up date plus the name or initials of the person requesting it. The original documents are filed in the normal filing system so that they are available if required before the follow-up date. The copy document is then placed in the follow-up folder for the month in which the follow-up is required.

When that month arrives the copy documents or 'tickler' forms are sorted into the days of the month and placed in the 1 to 31 sections. Each morning, the follow-ups for that day are taken out, married up with the documents required and passed to the person requesting them. A variation is simply to give the follow-up copies or forms to that person, who then selects the items for which the files are required. It relies on people remembering if a matter has been dealt with in the meantime, but they often do. This system saves the time of the person responsible for follow-ups because files are not taken out of the cabinets unnecessarily.

Competence Builder 9   *(Elements 12.1, 16.1, 17.1, 18.1, 21.1, 21.2)*

What type of follow-up system is in use in your organisation? Find out how to use it:

a) as a file user;

b) as a person who does the filing.

METHODS OF FILING FOLDERS

Finding records quickly when required is important and the filing method used should facilitate their swift retrieval. Vertical and lateral methods are common for the filing of folders: each has advantages, but also disadvantages which have to be accommodated.

Lateral Filing

The file folders are placed side-by-side on open shelves, in cupboards or are suspended in pockets from rails. The pockets are fitted with title holders which are sometimes angled to make it easier to read the file names. Difficulty in reading file names is one disadvantage of this method.

A further disadvantage arises from one of the advantages – the fact that filing shelves can be built right up to the ceiling. This saves space, but retrieving files from a height is a safety hazard which needs to be guarded against by using firm steps and taking care.

The major advantage of lateral filing, space saving, is further achieved because space does not have to be left to allow for the opening of drawers, as is the case with vertical filing.

Vertical Filing

The file folders are arranged, usually in cabinet drawers, so that they stand upright. Their titles can be seen clearly, and papers can be looked at or filed without removing the folders.

The file folders are however less likely to last a long time when stored in this way. Pockets are available, fitted together concertina fashion, which are suspended from metal runners fitted inside the drawers. Placing the folders inside these not only protects files and keeps them neat, but also provides a place for an absent marker when a file is borrowed.

There are also safety hazards to be guarded against with this type of filing. These arise from carelessness in leaving drawers open, which people might walk into or fall over, and opening more than one drawer at a time which can cause the cabinet to topple over.

METHODS OF FILING OTHER RECORDS

Sometimes records to be filed will not fit into a conventional file folder. These include large plans and drawings (for which drawers and specially fitted cabinets are available), computer printouts (for which special equipment is also available) and cards.

Card Filing

Cards are commonly used to provide an index for a filing system where direct access is difficult, for example, a numerical system. They are also used as filing systems in their own right. Stock records, accounts records, customer records and mailing lists are a few examples of the types of information which can be conveniently placed on cards.

When cards are not referred to frequently they can be filed vertically in a box or small drawer. If used frequently they can be placed more conveniently in rotating trays or fixed to the centre of a wheel which is easily rotated to bring the required card into view.

Visible Card Methods

A visible method is particularly convenient to use when cards have to be updated regularly and where a quick means of drawing attention to some of them from time-to-time is desired.

One piece of equipment used for a visible card method, which covers these requirements, consists of a number of flat trays contained within a metal cabinet. In the trays are overlapping card holders. The bottom edges of the cards are covered by a transparent plastic shield. The title of the card is written here, plus any other information which needs to be seen at a glance. The firm support given by the trays allows the cards to be written upon without the need to remove them from the card holder.

Strip indexes are useful for lists (telephone numbers, prices, etc.) which need to be referred to quickly and which are subject to change. They consist of 'pages' of strips which can be typed on, then separated and fitted into a frame, panel or multi-ring binder. Additions, deletions and amendments can be made rapidly without affecting the continuity of the records which are then always up-to-date.

Competence Builder 10 *(Element 12.1)*

If you worked through the Companion Level I Book, *Foundation Competences in Business Administration*, continue to add to your filing system. If not, then set up a personal filing system now. This will be used for storing the information you gather and produce as a result of working through the Competence Builders in this book.

Your personal set of files will be helpful for reference, and you will find it is worth adding to and using for a long time. Other useful sources of reference to include are personalised versions of some of the checklists in this book. Add leaflets and other information you collect from exhibitions and business magazines. If you have to prove some of your competences by means of a realistic simulation, or keep records over a period of time to show the external verifier, you can also use your filing system for keeping these papers.

If folders are not available, you may be able to obtain some large, used envelopes from the post room. These are usually thrown away. With new labels they provide a satisfactory means of keeping papers together.

Since you will be making an unknown quantity of additions to your files, the numerical system will be convenient. Use an alphabetical index and make cross-references. Although you will lose a major advantage of your filing system, i.e. a personal reference file, it might be more convenient for this Competence Builder to be carried out as a group project. In this case remember also to set-up a means of recording absent files.

COMPUTER DATA STORAGE

Computers are being used increasingly for storing records. People are becoming familiar with accessing them and because records are more readily available, information within the organisation can be used more advantageously for the development of its business. The computer takes filing beyond its basic purpose, that of storing and retrieving information.

This speedy and easy access to information, and easy updating, is of great benefit to computer users, but can be a danger to individuals whose personal data is recorded. The Data Protection Act 1984 was set-up to protect information about individuals stored on computer files and enforce a set of standards for the processing of such information (see page 49).

Competence Builder 11

(Element 12.1)

Research computerised filing. If available within your organisation ask to see and preferably do some work in connection with it. Alternatively, find an organisation where computerised filing is in operation and try to arrange a visit. Read about it.

Information Processing

In recent years computers have had a great impact on office work. Because they can store and process a large amount of data in a short period of time and therefore speed up work, they have become widely adopted for carrying out much routine, repetitive clerical work, including that in connection with:

▶ the payroll, where programs combine the calculation of wages and salaries with the updating of records;

▶ order processing, which in addition can include checking stock and producing documents for production;

▶ stock control, which can also carry out up-to-date costing and forecast demand;

▶ cash flow control, which in addition to recording the flow of cash in and out of a business can also record overdue debts and assist the forecasting of cash requirements;

▶ production control, which not only allows for the efficient scheduling of production and maintenance of equipment, but also calculates final output and provides mangement statistics.

The need for competency in this area of office work is underlined by the inclusion of information processing in all three options – Administrative, Financial and Secretarial – of the Business Administration National Vocational Qualification (NVQ) at Level II. In this NVQ, three elements have been identified as being necessary for competence in information processing:

1. Processing records in a database;

2. Processing information in spreadsheets;

3. Accessing and printing hard copy reports, summaries and documents.

To enable you to meet the requirements of each of these elements it is essential that you should be able to interpret oral and written instructions (including manuals), and be capable of safely operating, caring for, and maintaining, the equipment.

Competence Builder 1   *(Elements 13.1, 13.2, 13.3)*

Are you currently familiar with the equipment which will be available for you to use, in working towards competence in this Unit?

a) If you are not yet familiar with the equipment, negotiate with your boss or tutor an opportunity for you to see it in use, and at some stage be shown how to operate it. Ask to borrow the equipment manuals to see if you can understand them. Ask for clarification of anything which is unclear.

b) If you are familiar with the equipment check your knowledge of all aspects of operation, care and maintenance, and ensure that you can apply your knowledge. Check that you know what to do in the case of a fault occurring, and whom you should go to if you have other problems.

PROCESSING RECORDS IN A DATABASE

Databases are the computerised equivalents of card indexes and allow complex sorting of large stores of information. A typical card index might contain names and addresses with perhaps other information. Simply selecting a few records for a specific purpose from a large manual system takes time and there is always the possibility of misfiling to delay the work. Computer sorting is done in seconds.

Computer sorting can be by any of the details recorded or any combination of them. You can pull out specific groups of names, say people in a particular area with a particular interest and within a specified age range, to inform about an event taking place locally or a specialised item for sale. To do this manually would be a slow and tedious job, but is done quickly using a database package. Printouts can be in the form of self-adhesive labels, ready for dispatch, which saves the lengthy job of typing names and addresses.

Processing records in a database involves keeping the records up-to-date, i.e. creating new records, deleting and updating entries; copying data files to other disks, for example, for security; sorting records into alphabetical and numerical order; and searching and accessing specified data. When required to do any of this work you must always be alert to errors and correct them. This does require you to concentrate since errors on the screen are very easy to miss.

In order to satisfactorily process records in a database, or information in spreadsheets, you must be competent in interpreting manuscripts (realistically recognising that their quality can vary considerably); in keyboarding; and in proofreading screen and printed documents. You must also be familiar with business terminology, and be able to plan and organise your work in order to meet deadlines.

Competence Builder 2

(Elements 13.1, 13.2, 16.1, 17.1, 18.1, and in planning and organising work to meet deadlines)

Critically assess your own level of knowledge and skills in the areas stated in the last paragraph and agree an action plan with your boss or tutor for correcting any deficiencies. If you are not sure of your competence in any of these matters ask for an opinion.

Starting Up

Your first task is to load and access the computer system. You will be specifically shown how to do this on the equipment you will be required to use, but since the microcomputer is in common use, let us look at the starting-up procedure for this in order to see what is involved.

Before the computer can follow your instructions it needs to have a special auxiliary piece of software loaded onto it which will start the machine up. This is called the disk operating system (DOS), a program which like any other consists of a sequence of instructions. The difference is that without it the computer is unable to do anything useful because the programs you later use give instructions to, and pass information to and from, the disk operating system. It is involved in almost everything that happens in the computer.

Security

Access to systems and computer files, and the facility to enter data, is usually restricted. Authorised users are generally given confidential passwords which must be keyed in before the system can be accessed. Also, for security reasons, programs and files are kept locked away and are only issued to authorised users, with each occasion commonly being recorded in a register.

Competence Builder 3

(Elements 13.1, 13.2, 13.3)

If you do not already know, find out how to start up and close down the equipment you will be required to use. What security procedures must you observe?

Storing Records on Disks

In some cases, computers remember programs and the data typed into them only whilst they are switched on. The data disappears when the computer is switched off and must, therefore, be stored if it is wanted for future use. This is what disks are for. So called 'floppy' disks are used on the microcomputer. They do not appear to be 'floppy' because they are protected by a rigid plastic case, but they are susceptible to damage. Because they store magnetic fields they must be kept away from other magnetic sources, extremes of temperature are bad for them, as is any kind of dust or dirt. You should also avoid touching the small slot in the plastic covering through which the disk itself is visible, and never put anything on top or bend them. To prevent filing problems in storing disks always make sure that they are dated and labelled with names which not only clearly indicate what is on them, but which are also meaningful to other users.

Formatting

A new disk is magnetically blank and before it can be used must be formatted. This magnetises the disk coating on both sides with a series of concentric tracks, ready to receive the inputted information, and has been compared with laying down tracks on a record. All disks have to be formatted to the pattern recognised by the particular computer with which they are going to be used. Once a disk has been formatted it can be used for storage. You can also format an old disk if you want to clear it of everything saved on it. A word of caution – if you are going to format an old disk do check first that nothing stored on it is required. It is a dangerous command to issue unless you are certain of this fact.

Competence Builder 4   (Elements 13.1, 13.2)

Find out how to format disks and ask for an opportunity to practise carrying out this operation.

Input Devices

The keyboard is currently the main device for inputting information to a computer, but might, in due course, face much competition from voice input devices. The typical computer keyboard has the standard 'QWERTY' character keys, which you will recognise from using a typewriter, together with a number of special keys. These keys vary according to the make of computer, but are basically used to send commands to the computer.

Changing from a typewriter to a computer keyboard may seem difficult at first because of all the additional keypresses to learn. After some time however you will find that you become used to this change, and are well-pleased with all the additional functions available for enhancing and easing your work.

The 'mouse' is becoming common. It is a small object which sits on the desktop and which is controlled by hand. It has a ball protruding from its base and as you push the mouse over the surface of the desk the movements are detected by its internal mechanism and converted to electrical signals. These are fed into the computer via a wire and converted by the software to corresponding movements of the cursor across the screen. Most of these devices have two or three buttons which sit under your fingers as you rest your hand on the mouse.

The mouse has become popular as more computers use programs to simplify basic operations and these are displayed on the screen as a list from which options have to be selected. This is often easier with a mouse because all you have to do is point at a name on the screen and press the appropriate buttons to select the operation, such as renaming a file, that you want to perform. Moving rapidly from one point to another in a file of records, table of data, or a word-processed document is also easier using a mouse rather than the keyboard.

Data Files

A file is an organised collection of related records. An example would be a firm's employee records organised in alphabetical order. These records might include (in addition to people's names) their home addresses, telephone numbers, dates of birth, works' numbers, rates of pay and the names of the departments in which they work. These details could change, more records can be added and others deleted. This modifying of a file is called 'updating'.

	Record 1	Record 2	Record 3	Record N
Field 1 (Name)	Dyson Brian	Jones Roy	King Chris	Young Tony
Field 2 (Address)	2 St John St	70 Green St	11 Field Cres	9 Dean Rd
Field 3 (Tel no)	——	76149	52582	72471
Field 4 (Subscription – Sports Club)	——	75	——	——
Field 5 (Subscription – Union)	150	150	——	150
Field 6 (Holiday Fund)	300	——	500	——

Figure 5.1 Computer file

The records on the file in the example shown (see Figure 5.1) contain a number of separate items of data, for example, address, telephone number, etc. These subdivisions of a record are known as 'fields'. All records in a file must have the same number of fields and the data on each record must be in the same order. This means that if the first field of the first record holds the name of an employee, then it is in the first field of all other employee records that employees' names must appear. The second field of every record will similarly hold the same information about each employee, for example, home address, and so on. The same number of fields must exist for each record, even if some do not contain any data. This happens on records in the example (see Figure 5.1) where an employee does not have a home telephone or does not make certain voluntary payments.

You must think carefully when choosing names for files in order to ensure that you decide upon ones which will readily identify the files to all other users. Your choice might however be constrained by the file-naming rules of your organisation. If you are given your own choice keep your naming system consistent and memorable. Try and convey as much useful information as possible without becoming obscure and finishing up with a collection of numbers and letters, all of which mean something – but all of which are unmemorable! If for any reason you are not able to choose a name which conveys sufficient information regarding what is on the disks you could consider keeping an index showing the names together with more detail as to the file content.

Competence Builder 5

(Elements 13.1, 13.2)

a) Find out and keep a note of any file-naming rules in your organisation.

b) Acquaint yourself with the preferred styles and formats used in your organisation in regard to work you will be required to carry out. If appropriate make notes or copies for reference.

Backup Copies

It is a wise precaution to make backup copies automatically. If it is your decision to make, and you have the opportunity to backup a file, you should do so. As a general rule of thumb, you should save your work with a backup copy after you have entered an amount you would not like to have to redo. Do not be deceived into thinking that there is not much likelihood of anything happening to erase the work on the disk. Apart from your own error, which might accidentally erase some work, loss can be caused by a failure in the power supply or even a computer virus which afflicts the disk operating system!

In addition to saving work as you go along it is also advisable to make copies regularly of files which have to be kept for any period of time. This is to ensure that if the file you are working on becomes damaged there is a replacement. The duplicate file, provided it is kept physically separate, also ensures a replacement in case of loss by theft or fire. The extent to which you make copies and the frequency will of course depend upon the procedures laid down for your organisation.

Competence Builder 6

(Elements 13.1, 13.2)

a) Find out what your organisation's rules are regarding backup copies and duplicate files. If these are detailed, type a copy for reference.

b) Ask to be shown how to copy disks and negotiate opportunities for practice.

Networks

A network is the term used to describe several computers linked together in such a way that they can share software (such as databases) and hardware (such as printers); and even electronic mail (messages) is possible. Some networks have 'dumb' terminals. These are workstations with no processing power of their own and which have to rely on the host computer to carry out all the processing (host computers hold the files used by the other computers on the network). 'Intelligent' terminals possess their own processing power.

Competence Builder 7
(Element 13.1)

a) Using a standalone system or an 'intelligent' terminal attached to a network, and in real situations or realistic simulations, process records on a minimum of two commercial database files, for example, stock records and catalogues. You should carry out the following operations: load, access and close down the system; format disks; create new records; save/delete data entries; copy a data file to another disk; sort records into alphabetical and numerical order; and search and access specified data. Throughout you should be alert to any errors and ensure that they are corrected.

b) Over a period of time, check that you are meeting the following criteria:

▶ Data file formats always conform to defined specifications.

▶ New data files are correctly created, amended and deleted, as directed.

▶ Data is correctly transcribed and entered into correctly identified fields.

▶ All database files are without transcription error.

▶ Backup files are always produced and stored safely.

▶ Requested information is located, accessed and retrieved within specified time constraints.

▶ Security and confidentiality of information are always maintained.

▶ Faults and failures are identified and reported promptly.

▶ Operating and safety procedures are followed at all times.

In order to be assessed as competent you must meet all the above requirements.

The Data Protection Act 1984

This Act applies to anyone who has information about individuals on computer records. Basically, the purpose of the Act is to protect people with names and facts about them on computers from having that information used in ways detrimental to their interests.

The Act gives individuals the right to find out what information is held about them on computer files. They can write to the owners of these files (the data users) for a copy of this information, apply for any inaccuracies to be corrected, and claim compensation through the courts for any damage or distress suffered as a result of inaccuracy, through an unlawful disclosure, or by the loss or destruction of personal data. If there is any objection to the way in which an organisation is collecting or using data, complaints can be made to the Data Protection Registrar.

Any user of data to which the Act applies must have registered their use of such data with the Data Protection Registrar and comply with the Data Protection Principles. The guidelines to the Act state that personal data must be:

▶ obtained and processed fairly and lawfully;

▶ held only for the lawful purposes specified in the register entry;

▶ used only for those purposes and only be disclosed to those people described in the register entry;

▶ adequate, relevant and not excessive in relation to the purpose for which it is held;

▶ accurate and, where necessary, kept up-to-date;

▶ held no longer than is necessary for the stated purpose;

▶ made accessible to the individuals named and, where appropriate, corrected or erased;

▶ surrounded by appropriate security to guard against unauthorised access, alteration, disclosure or destruction, or accidental loss or destruction.

The last point above is particularly important in that it underlines the importance of adhering to security rules. The provisions of the Data Protection Act apply to the everyday activities you might be asked to carry out. If you are negligent, you and your organisation could be in breach of the Act. Someone within your organisation must be appointed to handle all details arising from the Act and it is to this person you should turn with any queries.

Competence Builder 8   *(Elements 12.1, 13.1)*

Find out who has been appointed in your organisation to be responsible for handling matters concerning the Data Protection Act. If there is anything you do not understand with regard to the Act ask this person.

PROCESSING INFORMATION IN SPREADSHEETS

Spreadsheet packages are an extremely useful aid in planning and decision making because you can calculate instantly the consequences of alternative courses of action. This 'what-if?' facility can be used to show, for example, the effect if costs increase by a certain percentage or if sales fall by a stated amount. The new data is simply fed into the pre-existing spreadsheet leaving the other data unchanged, and the answers immediately appear.

Spreadsheets are not however confined to providing this type of managerial aid. They are flexible programs which can be used for any application the user requires and, in particular, where you want to carry out calculations automatically on tables and figures. Common examples of their use are for budgeting, cash-flow forecasts, stock control, and job and contract costing.

The simplification of budgets and forecasts was the original idea behind computerised spreadsheets. The manual way of doing this consists of using a sheet of paper divided up into rows and columns and then filling in the resulting boxes with numbers. Alterations entail several lots of rubbing out and overwriting which is time-consuming and leads to a messy final result.

Competence Builder 9
(Element 13.2)

Find out what spreadsheets are used for in your organisation. To what extent have these speeded up work previously done manually? To what new applications have spreadsheets been applied?

Spreadsheets organise data in the form of a table or worksheet. The worksheet is divided vertically into columns which are usually identified by letters, A, B and so on. The worksheet is also divided horizontally into rows which are numbered downwards starting at 1. The cells (the name for the spreadsheet data entry boxes in the grid) are identified by the column letter and row number in which they lie, for example, in Figure 5.2 the cell lying at the intersection of column B and row 3 is called B3.

Besides data, a cell can contain a programming statement or formula. These are not visible when you are typing in data but they are there, waiting to perform

	A	B	C	D	E
1		Jan	Feb	Mar	Apr
2					
3	Sales	1600	1700	1500	1800
4	Less				
5	Purchases	600	700	500	800
6	Expenses	400	300	300	400
7					
8	Total	1000	1000	800	1200
9					
10	Profit	600	700	700	600

Figure 5.2 Cash budget spreadsheet

	A	B	C	D	E
1		Jan	Feb	Mar	Apr
2					
3	Sales	1600	1700	1500	1800
4	Less				
5	Purchases	600	700	500	800
6	Expenses	400	300	300	400
7					
8	Total	B5 + B6	C5 + C6	D5 + D6	E5 + E6
9					
10	Profit	B3 − B8	C3 − C8	D3 − D8	E3 − E8

Figure 5.3 Spreadsheet showing underlying formulae

mathematical calculations on the contents of the other cells. When this is acted on, the result is inserted in the cell which contains the formula. For example, in the cell at the bottom of a row you can enter a formula stating what calculation is to be carried out using the numbers above it (see Figure 5.3). The calculation is automatically carried out and the answer appears in the box as can be seen in Figure 5.2. If any of the numbers are then changed the formula will be automatically applied to show the revision, i.e. when any of the numbers in the row are changed the number at the bottom changes too.

Spreadsheets are set-up and modified using a menu of commands which appear on the screen. Words and numbers can then be entered, as can formulae. One useful command allows you to copy the structure of one cell, such as a complicated formula, to other cells. You can also copy entire rows or columns. This is useful if, for example, you are setting up a spreadsheet for the month of the year, with the basic structure for each month being the same. Some spreadsheet packages will also convert ranges of numbers into graphs which convey the information more vividly than numbers ever can.

Competence Builder 10 *(Element 13.2)*

a) If you are competent in the Competence Builder 7 operations, but are not yet familiar with the work involved in processing information in spreadsheets, ask to be shown on a spreadsheet package with automatic options how to: create new spreadsheets; search/sort and access relevant areas of the spreadsheet; and carry out automatic calculations (incorporating the automatic manipulation of data).

b) If/when you are familiar with processing information in spreadsheets, negotiate opportunities to build up your competence. As applies when your competence is being assessed, you can use a standalone system or an 'intelligent' terminal attached to a network and carry out the work in a real situation or realistic simulation. You must aim for competence in the operations stated in Competence Builder 10a).

You will know that it is time to ask for your competence to be assessed in processing information in spreadsheets when your work meets the following performance criteria:

▶ spreadsheet formats always conform to defined specifications;
▶ spreadsheets are correctly created, amended and deleted as directed;
▶ data is correctly transcribed and entered into correctly identified files;
▶ all spreadsheets are without transcription error;
▶ backup files are always produced and stored safely;
▶ projections are correctly generated, as directed;
▶ security and confidentiality of information is always maintained;
▶ faults/failures are identified and reported promptly;
▶ operating and safety procedures are followed at all times.

ACCESSING AND PRINTING HARD COPY MATERIAL

Computer printers come in a variety of shapes and sizes, and also vary in their capabilities in so far as text enhancements, such as underlining and emboldening are concerned, and their ability to print graphics. The speed of the printer available has to be considered in planning your work. They tend to cause bottle-necks in computer operations because their mechanical apparatus cannot keep up with the speed of the electronic processing. For hard copy output (paper printouts) the main types of printer are dot matrix, daisywheel and laser.

Dot matrix printers are flexible, can handle any kind of paper (continuous and single sheet) and being inexpensive have proved popular. A problem with dot matrix printouts is that the images, which are built up in layers of dots, look as though they have come out of a computer and are not always considered to be of a high enough quality. This has been overcome to some extent by printer manufacturers who have produced machines which offer a near letter quality (NLQ) mode. When in this mode the print head prints each line twice, the second printing slightly offset from the first and thus filling in the gaps between the dots. The quality is more acceptable but the printing speed is reduced.

Daisywheel printers use a method of printing which is identical to that used for many typewriters. The print quality is therefore high and this is their major advantage. Unlike dot matrix printers they cannot print graphics and the daisywheel has to be changed if you want to change the type style, or print special symbols or foreign language characters. Like the dot matrix they are noisy and are generally slower.

Laser printers resemble a photocopier in size and appearance, the technology is similar and, as with photocopying, an entire page is produced at a time. They are quieter than the impact printers (dot matrix and daisywheel) and faster. The quality is good and they can print high-quality graphics. Many however will only print single sheets of A4 paper and are therefore unsuited to printing out long horizontal documents such as spreadsheets. On the whole they require more maintenance and tend to be more expensive than the impact printers.

Competence Builder 11 *(Element 13.3)*

a) Discuss the use of the printer available to you with your boss, tutor or whoever shows you how to use it. Find out if there are any maintenance procedures which you have to follow and what print problems can arise. Which of these, if any, are you expected to deal with yourself? What problems should you refer and to whom?

b) Research and make notes for your reference file on: inkjet printers, thermal printers and colour printing.

Effective Use of Resources

In order to work effectively you must know what software and hardware resources are available to you, and be knowledgeable about the capabilities and facilities of the equipment, and the various programs available. This should ensure that when you are asked to carry out work you will be able to plan it so that the result is that desired by the originator. You will also be in a position to make suggestions for matching what is desired with what is possible and available.

Competence Builder 12

(Element 13.3)

Negotiate opportunities in a real situation or realistic simulation to print hard copy reports, summaries and documents. You should ask for instruction and practise carrying out the following operations:

▶ accessing and closing down the system;

▶ loading the printer and setting the print specification; and

▶ replenishing the paper feed.

In all your work, ensure that the information is correctly accessed by document/record/field, that all printed output conforms to the specification, and that documents are correctly collated and distributed as directed.

Telecommunications and Data Transmission

People who work in offices can expect to spend a lot of time on the telephone. It is a much used and abused method of communication. Used well it offers a cost-effective, immediate means of giving and receiving information. Used badly it is an expensive, time-consuming source of frustration.

OPERATING A MULTILINE OR SWITCHBOARD SYSTEM

You might be required to operate a multiline or switchboard system, as an integral part of your job, or to act as a relief operator. In order to be competent in this role you must be aware of acceptable telephone techniques and be able to use them automatically. You must also be able to communicate effectively and without unnecessary waffle. You are not required to be chatty. Everyone recognises that brevity is essential if telephone costs are to be kept down, and it is perfectly possible and acceptable to be brief without giving the impression that matters are not being dealt with adequately or politely.

Competence Builder 1

(Element 14.1)

a) Cost the following telephone calls:

   i) 4 minute local calls at peak, standard and cheap rates;

   ii) 4 minute **a** band calls at peak, standard and cheap rates;

   iii) 4 minute **b** band calls at peak, standard and cheap rates;

b) Draw up a chart or charts to emphasise the differing costs established in a) above.

c) What time periods do peak, standard and cheap rates apply to?

d) Find out from your local British Telecom phone book the places you can telephone at low cost **b1** charge band rates. Make a note of these on the telephone charges information to which you would refer when required to cost calls.

Telephone Manner

When you are speaking on the telephone at work you are looked upon as your organisation's representative. If you are curt or rude then an unfavourable image of the organisation is formed. If you are courteous and considerate then the image of the organisation is enhanced.

When people visit an organisation there are a number of props available to promote a caring image of the organisation to the visitor; magazines, comfortable chairs, courtesies which add to the visitor's comfort, the receptionist's welcoming manner and words. When speaking on the telephone these props are not visible and your voice is all you have for creating a good impression. How you use your voice is all important. Your tone should be cheerful, warm and friendly, and your manner considerate and sympathetic. A word of caution though – be friendly but not over-familiar. Business relationships and communications are becoming less formal, but the degree of informality acceptable varies from one person to another, and from one organisation to another.

A business relationship has to be allowed to develop in the same way as friendships develop – at a speed and to a level acceptable to both parties. A lessening of formality will often occur naturally after meeting face-to-face someone previously only known as a telephone contact. This is because you are better able to visualise a person's response, and thus judge more precisely the appropriate tone and manner to adopt. This cannot be done at the outset however and it is wise to be cautious. An approach which is businesslike without being curt, which conveys a willingness to help, combined with a sound knowledge of the job, will assure people that the call is being dealt with efficiently.

Telephone Speech

Clarity is essential when speaking on the telephone and you should try to develop a good speaking voice. This means that there must be no slurred consonants, flattened vowels or running of words and sentences together. You should sound calm, relaxed and unhurried. Speak slowly but not in a laboured manner, emphasise consonants and enunciate clearly. Neither shout nor whisper. Make sure you put expression into your voice. Speaking in a dull monotone is boring to listen to and this can be enlivened by modulating the voice, i.e. changing its pitch. If a sentence is started in a low pitch the voice will rise naturally and can be brought down again for the next sentence or comment. The female voice, being generally higher pitched, should be deliberately pitched lower for telephone use.

Words with the same vowel sound, such as five and nine, can sound alike and special care has to be taken when quoting figures, names and unfamiliar words. When necessary, spell out place names or words difficult to understand, using the telephone alphabet.

If the listener cannot hear it is preferable to speak more distinctly rather than more loudly. The hand cupped round the mouthpiece helps. At all times one should speak straight into the mouthpiece, not across it as this distorts the sound and allows background noise to be heard.

You should not eat or drink whilst using the telephone. Avoid slang such as 'Okay', 'Right-oh', 'Half-a-tick' and 'Tarrah', and never address people as 'Love', 'Me duck', or similar.

Use phrases and statements which sound pleasant and helpful rather than curt and slangy. For example, 'One moment please', rather than 'Hang on'; 'I'm sorry but Mr Dicer is not in the office at the moment', rather than 'He's out'; 'Could you repeat that please?', rather than 'What's that?'.

Competence Builder 2   *(Elements 14.1, 15.1, 19.1, 19.2)*

a) Find a copy of a telephone alphabet and either photocopy, write or type a copy for your own use.

b) Roleplay a number of telephone calls during which it becomes necessary to use the telephone alphabet, until you are able to do so automatically.

c) During your telephone conversations, of whatever kind, make a note of the expressions people use which sound abrupt and unfriendly. Keep the note by you and make sure that you avoid these and similar expressions.

Processing Incoming Calls

▶ When receiving a direct outside call, unless the policy of the organisation differs, give its name first, for example 'Matthews and Hope', so that the caller knows immediately that the right number has been obtained. 'Good morning' or 'Good afternoon' can follow.

▶ Always answer a call promptly. Once answered it must then be dealt with. Apart from the unnecessary expense, any delay might be an inconvenience for the caller, especially for someone in a callbox with a limited amount of change or a phonecard with very few units left on it.

▶ You should expect callers to identify themselves immediately. Some do not and tend to start a conversation straight away. Do not interrupt the caller but obtain their name as soon as there is a pause.

▶ Establish the caller's requirements as soon as possible. 'Buzz' the person for whom the call is intended and put the call through if requested to do so.

▶ Where you cannot meet a caller's request, for whatever reason, always be courteous and helpful. Try to find out and offer the option(s) available.

▶ Never attempt to listen in and do not repeat anything overheard accidentally. There must be no doubt about your being able to treat matters confidentially, either those officially entrusted or those happened upon by chance.

▶ Deal with queries speedily. Knowing from where information can be obtained and who deals with what, gives an impression not only of personal efficiency but of efficiency of the organisation as a whole. You must know, therefore, the location and responsibilities of people in the organisation.

Competence Builder 3

(Element 14.1)

a) In a real situation or realistic simulation of an office environment, operate a multiline or switchboard system including:

▶ identifying and establishing the needs of callers;

▶ connecting callers to correct internal lines.

b) If your switchboard experience is limited, obtain approval to make a list, from discussion with the regular operator, of the types of queries which have to be dealt with. Draw up a chart of your organisation with telephone extension numbers. Cross-reference the list with the chart so that you have a general idea of who deals with each type of query. Keep this in your file.

On-hold and Transfer Calls

If a call has to be left for an enquiry to be made or some information found, then the caller should be informed how long this is likely to take, and be given the opportunity to call back in a stated length of time. This avoids unnecessary costs being incurred and also prevents snippets of conversations being overheard. If it is not practical for the caller to call back then the telephone must be adequately 'muffled'. Some systems play music whilst callers are on 'hold', but calling back or being called back is the best alternative. It saves money and the inconvenience to others of lines being engaged. When a caller is going to 'hold on' do not place the receiver heavily on the table or desk, or leave it to dangle. This can cause damage to the instrument, and a loud bang or the tapping of a dangling receiver is not pleasant to hear.

Callers are impressed if they are transferred competently. Incompetence can result in contact being lost, and the caller left in limbo to get more and more agitated. It is equally irritating for a caller to be transferred and retransferred, and you must not be guilty of this.

Competence Builder 4

(Element 14.1)

a) In a real situation or realistic simulation operate a switchboard/multiline system and:

▶ transfer calls to alternative internal extensions;

▶ deal with a misdirected or wrong number;

▶ deal with a caller who has been passed around from one person to another and is becoming irate.

b) Find out about, and keep a note for reference of, common faults on equipment, their symptoms and the corrective action recommended.

Dealing with Complaints

People often behave more aggressively on the telephone than face-to-face. Sometimes this is because it is easy to misjudge a response when the other person's reactions cannot be seen. Sometimes it is because people feel braver knowing that a call can be terminated if it becomes too difficult.

People telephoning to make a complaint frequently assume an aggressive manner because they want to ensure that the matter gets attention. Their aggression lessens if they feel that they are being listened to carefully. In dealing with such cases, be sympathetic but never acknowledge responsibility or argue against the person's complaint. When you are on the switchboard you are merely trying to find out enough in order to pass the caller on promptly to the best person able to settle the matter.

Never reciprocate with bad temper when dealing with irate people. It only causes further aggravation. Staying calm helps to cool the situation and you gain satisfaction from having kept your self-control.

Some telephone calls do not run smoothly and you must be prepared for people who are rude, impatient or unpleasant in some other way. Just be determined to be pleasant and polite yourself, bearing in mind that the words you use and the tone you adopt affect the other person's response.

Tact and Diplomacy

Tact and diplomacy is needed in handling the varied situations that arise on the telephone. This is especially so when the person in the organisation asked for declines to accept a call. When informing the caller of this, the impression given should be that the call would be taken if it were at all possible.

Sometimes callers refuse to give a name. This might be because they know that a call from them is unlikely to be accepted. A polite but firm refusal to pass on such a call saying, 'I'm sorry but she will not speak to anyone who has not given their name', is reasonable.

Operating a switchboard can include the requirement to screen calls, i.e. to find out not only the person's name and company but also some indication of the subject they are phoning about. This policy is likely if there are frequent occasions when people ask to speak to a certain person about matters with which others could adequately deal. You will need to be diplomatic so that people do not feel that they are getting second best.

Meetings are not normally interrupted by telephone calls nor should a person be disturbed when they are dealing with an important visitor. That person's secretary or colleague will usually take a message and hand it over afterwards.

Tact is also needed on occasions when it is necessary to 'cover up' for someone, albeit for a legitimate reason! Callers should not be told, 'X is not back from lunch yet', especially in the middle of the afternoon, or 'Y hasn't arrived yet'. Both give a bad impression and there might be perfectly legitimate reasons why the people asked for are not at their desks. It is sufficient to say, 'X is not in the office at the moment'. An offer for the caller to speak to someone else or to leave a message can be made.

You should know the organisation's policy with regard to whether or not you offer to telephone callers back or ask them to do so. If it depends upon the caller's status then take care. This is a policy which demands difficult decision making and could lead to problems.

If a call becomes disconnected during a conversation it is up to the call initiator to ring again. Following this rule ensures that both parties are not ringing each other simultaneously, thus finding the lines engaged.

Some organisations do not allow its telephone operators to take messages. The usual reason is that a switchboard is busy and taking messages can delay calls, both in and out. You have to be very tactful in refusing to take a message because it does sound very unhelpful to the caller. You must, therefore, try particularly hard to be helpful in other ways, such as suggesting when would be the best time for the caller to try again. It will be of help to you if someone could be named in your organisation who could take a message in an emergency, or who could deal with a caller with whom you are having difficulty over this aspect.

Competence Builder 5

(Element 14.1)

Unless you have regular opportunities for handling business calls from all kinds of people in a variety of situations, roleplay telephone calls using a switchboard or multiline system, from:

a) Callers who have got the wrong number.

b) Callers who are pressing very hard for information which must not be divulged, for example, about the organisation or personal details of employees.

c) Callers with seemingly justified complaints.

d) Callers with seemingly unjustified complaints.

e) Callers who ask for people by name but their call could be dealt with more adequately by someone else.

f) Callers who refuse to give their names.

g) Callers who ask for a certain person in the organisation who declines to speak to them.

Produce supporting evidence, in the form of logged action, for a minimum of ten calls

Messages

If you are allowed to take messages whilst working as the telephone operator then you must save time by responding to this request automatically.

Facts should be written down immediately, otherwise a message may be forgotten or important details omitted. For this purpose many organisations use pre-printed forms. These need to be kept where they are immediately available, either on the desk or on the top of a drawer. If you are right-handed, place the telephone message forms on your right-hand side; the opposite applies if you are left-handed. Read messages back before concluding the call in order to confirm accuracy. Ensure that messages are placed prominently on the desks of the people for whom they are intended so that they are seen as soon as possible.

Competence Builder 6

(Elements 14.1, 15.1)

Whilst operating a switchboard or multiline system, in a real situation or realistic simulation, take a variety of messages including those from:

▶ callers who do not volunteer information readily;

▶ foreign callers who are not easy to understand.

Pass messages on, some written, some oral, to the intended recipients.

Processing Outgoing Calls

▶ Efficient use of the telephone requires the effective use of British Telecom directories (including *Yellow Pages*), internal directories and codes. As a time-saver, draw up an index of regularly-called telephone numbers, together with relevant dialling codes.

▶ When operating a switchboard or multiline system obtain calls as quickly as possible. There will sometimes be delays outside your control. Keep your patience with anyone who constantly 'buzzes' if a number is taking a long time to obtain. Calmly state the reason for the delay, for example, the switchboard may be busy or the number required is engaged, and reassure them that you are doing your best on their behalf.

▶ If a wrong number is obtained, give only a brief apology before hanging up. It is rude not to apologise but equally annoying to the other person to be given a long explanation.

Competence Builder 7   *(Element 14.1)*

a) Familiarise yourself with the local telephone directory information pages. Check upon how to obtain local, national and international calls.

b) Familiarise yourself with *Yellow Pages* and any other classified directories which might be available. When might you use these?

c) Type instructions for reference on:

   i) How to contact the operator, emergency services or directory enquiries;

   ii) Use Freefone and Telemessage services.

   iii) Your organisation's policy on security, safety and emergencies, for example, bomb threats.

d) Find out the purpose of services such as alarm calls and fixed-time calls. Obtain for reference, the information leaflet regarding these and other operator services (see the telephone directory).

e) Compile a frequently-used telephone numbers' index for business or personal use including codes. Choose a suitable format for this.

f) Using a switchboard or multiline system, in a real situation or realistic simulation:

  ▶ obtain correct outside lines;

  ▶ establish priorities between calls;

  ▶ connect an international call;

  ▶ diagnose and report any switchboard faults which might occur;

  ▶ carry-out the routine cleaning of equipment.

Produce supporting evidence in the form of logged action for at least five calls.

TRANSMITTING AND TRANSCRIBING RECORDED MESSAGES

Telephone answering machines are in common use for taking messages when there is no one to answer a telephone. An outgoing message is recorded on the machine to inform the caller that the telephone is unattended but a message can be left. The outgoing message should state the organisation's name and telephone number, plus an apology that there is no one to answer the call at that time. This is then followed by an invitation to the caller to leave his or her name, telephone number and a message.

When you have to record a message, write it out first. Practise reading and timing it to ensure that you will not make an error, and that its length is not more than that permitted for an announcement (see the machine manual). When recording, speak clearly and at a normal speed. Try to sound friendly and encouraging because people tend not to like speaking to a machine and you want to prevent their hanging-up without leaving a message.

If you are responsible for taking calls, then any messages recorded should be listened to as soon as you return to your desk. The recorded messages must be transcribed accurately, with urgent messages identified and prioritised. All messages should be dealt with or passed on, as appropriate, without delay. Reset the answering machine immediately. Make sure that you follow the instructions you have been given regarding the keeping of messages on tapes after they have been transcribed. Sometimes, two or three tapes are rotated which means that messages are available for a short time for rechecking if it appears that an error, for example, in transcribing a telephone number, has been made.

If you are responsible for checking that the machine is always switched on when the office is unoccupied take care never to forget. Should a fault develop in the equipment, report it promptly, and in common with all your other duties make sure that you follow correct operating and safety procedures at all times.

Competence Builder 8 *(Element 14.2)*

In a real situation or realistic simulation, operate an answering machine including:

a) Composing and recording the message which gives instructions to the caller.

b) Setting-up the machine to record calls automatically and closing it down.

c) Playing back messages and passing them on to the people concerned, both orally and on a message form. These should include:

▶ routine and non-routine messages;

▶ incomplete messages requiring instant action;

▶ long messages requiring editing.

d) Leaving messages on an answering machine. This should include a message for someone to follow which will enable you to know whether or not your instructions were clear.

TRANSMITTING AND RECEIVING COPIES OF DOCUMENTS ELECTRONICALLY

You need to be aware of the range of communications services now available and their relative costs. Even if it is not part of the normal duties of your job, learning how to use systems which are available in your organisation, for example, telex, facsimile transmission and electronic mail, extends the areas in which you are competent both for work purposes and for gaining your qualifications.

Telex, the British Telecom teleprinter communication service, has been in operation many years. Dialling the correspondent's telex number establishes a link, the message is typed on a teleprinter and appears in printed form on both the sender's and the correspondent's machines.

You can use a facsimile transmission (fax) machine to send exact copies of documents, diagrams and other graphic material, as well as text, to anywhere connected by telephone. Fax is thus more versatile than telex. Fax machines have been available for many years. Reduced costs and transmission times, and increased reliability and quality have led to the dramatic growth of fax and it is becoming a common feature of business communications. Some machines are also used as photocopiers.

Electronic mail is run using a modem, a small electronic device which enables you to send information from one computer to another down a telephone line. Some computers have built-in modems. Software is used to organise the communication and information flows, and electronic mail can be integrated into systems with computer-based data processing, filing and retrieval.

You can expect someone to show you how to use the equipment, but should acquaint yourself with the equipment manuals so that you can refer to these if in doubt. Ask what records have to be completed to log equipment usage, and what maintenance and cleaning procedures have to be carried out routinely. Find out if you have to follow safety procedures specific to the use of the equipment and to whom you report any faults.

Competence Builder 9

(Element 14.3)

Do you have equipment in your organisation for transmitting and receiving documents electronically? If so, and you are not already using it, ask your boss or tutor if someone can teach you, and allow time for practice.

One of the Business Administration Level II NVQ elements requires proven competence on operational systems using any two of telex, fax or electronic mail. If not part of your normal duties this will have to be negotiated.

When you are practising, and indeed in your work, you should strive to meet the criteria against which your performance will be judged. Namely:

► The copies dispatched and received are always of acceptable quality.

► Accurate material only is dispatched.

► All outgoing material is transmitted to correct destinations.

► All incoming material is delivered promptly to correct locations.

► Records are up-to-date, legible and accurate.

► Faults are identified and reported promptly.

► Operating and safety procedures are followed at all times

You must be able to deal with documents of varying size and complexity, both in transmitting and receiving, and know how to make an international transmission. You must also know the appropriate corrective action to take when there appears to be a problem, for example, a wrongly-received transmission. In addition to operating the equipment, you need to be able to make effective use of available UK and foreign directories, and know the procedures for obtaining new codes, numbers and answerback codes (as appropriate to the equipment) from British Telecom and/or other suppliers.

Competence Builder 10   *(Element 14.3)*

a) In a real situation or realistic simulation using the equipment available to you:

   ▶ make an international transmission;

   ▶ deal with the following contingencies:
      i)   a wrongly received transmission;
      ii) a request to repeat an outgoing transmission;
      iii) a request for an incoming transmission to be repeated.

b) Find out how to use the directories relevant to your equipment.

c) Ask the regular operator of the equipment what things are most likely to go wrong and how these can be corrected.

d) Compare telex, facsimile and electronic mail, including transmission costs. Present this in a suitable format.

e) List appropriate occasions for the use of the telecommunications and data equipment available in your organisation. State the factors you have considered. Be prepared to justify your choices.

Reception

Many people working in business administration have contact with visitors to their organisation. Some undertake formal reception duties for a large proportion of their time, or occasionally on a rota system. Where an office worker's duties do not include formal reception work there are nevertheless occasions when visitors have to be met. When people arrive for a meeting, for example, someone has to greet them and be welcoming; customers and suppliers have to be seen. It may be necessary to see a visitor on behalf of someone else, or greet, escort and introduce a visitor to the boss. The tasks associated with receiving and directing visitors are ones, therefore, in which you should expect to demonstrate competence, particularly if you intend to specialise in administrative or secretarial work.

Competence in maintaining the reception area is also expected. You may currently have no responsibility for this but may have at some later time in your working life. You might, for example, work for a small organisation as the sole administrator or be the supervisor for a number of staff, including those working on reception.

The number of visitors to organisations varies as does the size and type of the reception area. This is immaterial because the basic tasks and, therefore, the competences needed, are common.

RECEIVING AND DIRECTING VISITORS

People visit organisations for different reasons – as customers, suppliers, colleagues and members of committees. Whatever the reason for their visits they are likely to be greeted at first by a receptionist or someone fulfilling this function. This person is the one from whom visitors receive first impressions of the organisation. Someone with a bright, friendly, helpful manner will immediately convey a good impression, as will a bright, cheery reception area. Conversely, an uncared for and uncaring person in a scruffy reception area could give the same impression of the organisation's products or services.

Appearance

A good impression is given by a good total appearance. This includes well-cared-for and well-fitting clothes, accessories which blend in and understated jewellery. Women require a minimum of makeup and men a daily shave or tidy beard/moustache. Both must have scrupulously clean hands, nails, teeth and skin; good personal hygiene; clean hair arranged in an attractive style; and good posture and graceful movements.

It is impossible to state what type of clothes you should wear because they must fit in with your working environment and work duties. In certain jobs there is what might be described as a uniform, an accepted mode of dress. If you are on reception duty in a solicitor's office, for example, you will be expected to be dressed more formally than if you are working in a beauty parlour or leisure centre. The image has to be appropriate whether it be conservative, glamorous or casual.

A good image is also to do with the way you walk, sit, use your hands and face, and how you smile. Your voice is another aspect of the image you project and is something which is noticed immediately. If you wish, it can be improved without doing anything drastic, like trying to assume a different accent. This is unnecessary as regional ones are acceptable and frequently admired.

Shrillness or low growls should, however, be modified, aiming for a middle of the range tone. It is important that the final result is natural. Making a tape recording helps in analysing how you sound, but remember that machines tend to emphasise accents. Working on the voice or anything which you might wish to change is always safer if someone else is available to give an honest opinion.

Competence Builder 1 *(Elements 10.1, 10.2, 15.1, 15.2)*

Critically assess your total business image. Better still ask a friend or colleague whom you can trust to offer constructive criticism. Can improvements be made?

Qualities

You will find certain qualities useful and worth developing: tact and courtesy for helping a visitor to feel comfortable; poise and flexibility for helping you to adapt to differing circumstances; firmness for occasions when social niceties have to be balanced with the need to keep things moving; and the ability to 'tune' in quickly.

You will also find that every visitor is different – some are quiet, some chatty, some pleasant, some curt – but whatever their attitude all must be treated as guests. You should always adopt a manner that presents a favourable image of the organisation and you must be able to deal with any difficulties which arise without prejudicing this.

If you are working on reception it is important to greet visitors immediately they arrive and not keep them hanging around. Even if you are speaking on the telephone at the time it is still possible to nod and smile to acknowledge their arrival. Under no circumstances should a visitor be ignored whilst you continue chatting to a colleague or carry on with a trivial task. Apart from the bad impression this creates you might be required quickly to give advice as to where the visitor can park. You should use a form of greeting laid down or accepted by your organisation, and once you have established a person's name continue to use it.

Next you must find out the reason for the visit. This sounds like a simple task, but is not always so. People are often not sure what they want or who they want to see, and do not always express their wishes clearly. You will find that your questioning skills are essential.

Appointments

Visitors fall naturally into two groups: those with, and those without, appointments.

Visitors' appointments should have been recorded in the appropriate diaries and their visits will thus be known about in advance. You, or the person who is on reception duty, should then be told each day who will be calling and at what time. Such visitors can then be welcomed as people who are expected and announced by telephone to the correct person.

Quite often people selling a product or service turn up in person because they have been unsuccessful in obtaining an appointment by other means. You must follow the organisation's rules for dealing with these visitors and this will include questioning them on the reason for their call. You can then ask them to write in for an appointment, or ask an appropriate person if he or she is free to see the visitor, depending on the laid down procedure. A personal assistant or executive level secretary might act as a 'filter' in these cases to judge whether or not the person asked for would wish to give an interview or if it is more appropriate for someone else to deal with the matter.

Some visitors turn up without an appointment because they are well-known business associates. Others do so for a variety of reasons, such as being in the area and having free time, but without sufficient notice to request an appointment.

If a caller turns up without an appointment he or she is usually willing to wait in order to be seen by an appropriate person. If there will be delay you should give a reason and, where possible, some indication of how long this might be. Then, depending on what is usual in your organisation, you can offer to hang up the visitor's hat or coat, offer a magazine or newspaper to read, and a cup of tea or coffee.

When people arrive unexpectedly there will inevitably be occasions when they cannot be seen or they have not time to wait. In such cases you can make an appointment for another day (after consultation with the appropriate member of staff) or you might take a message (see page 61). Every visitor should be treated courteously and be dealt with patiently, regardless of whether they are important or not, or have an appointment or not. What matters is that when they leave, even if they have not been seen, they are satisfied with their treatment and retain a good impression of the organisation.

You may have to deal with the receipt of deliveries when on reception duty and should do so in the appropriate manner (see page 113).

Competence Builder 2

(Elements 15.1, 15.2)

In a real situation and/or in roleplay deal with the following:

a) A visitor who wishes to leave a spoken message.

b) Visitors without appointments with matters to be dealt with which are:
   ▶ urgent;
   ▶ non-urgent.

c) Visitors with appointments who are:
   ▶ early;
   ▶ late.

d) A caller without an appointment who knows the name of the person required, but that person is not available or does not wish to see the caller.

e) A caller who has no appointment and refuses to disclose the reason for his or her visit.

f) A caller without an appointment who asks to see someone who would not be the best person to deal with the matter.

g) The receipt of a delivery of stationery. You do not inspect the contents.

Emergencies and Problems

Sometimes the person on reception duty has to deal with 'emergency' situations, such as someone's car being parked where it is causing an obstruction. What action you take depends on who or where the visitor is. If a meeting has to be interrupted, for example, then it might be prudent to send in a note stating the problem and suggesting that the car keys be sent out with the messenger. These can then be returned when the visitor leaves, together with a note stating where the car has been moved to.

Another type of problem arises when the person a visitor has called to see has forgotten the appointment or is dealing with some urgent matter which cannot be left. In these cases the visitor must be apologised to, and be offered a drink and reading material. Even if the visitor has been forgotten, it is tactful to state that the member of staff has been unavoidably delayed, since being overlooked can be regarded as an insult.

Sometimes irate people arrive demanding to see a particular person or to be dealt with immediately. Such people are indeed best dealt with as soon as possible since they tend to become more irate as time passes without their demands being attended to. They can create difficulties and you should know on whom to call for help in such circumstances.

Aim to develop the ability to recognise physical communication signals (i.e. body language) which indicate how people are feeling. This will help you to be more responsive in assisting people and also helps in recognising potentially aggressive individuals. You can make your leisure time work for you by looking for these signs when watching television. Notice, for example, how people unconsciously clench their fists and raise their voices when they are feeling angry, and how they poke their heads forward and wag their forefingers in people's faces.

Competence Builder 3 *(Elements 15.1, 15.2)*

a) In a real situation or in roleplay, deal with the following:

▶ a visitor who is not very good at stating what he or she has come about, and does not know whom to ask for;

▶ a visitor who has a complaint and becomes aggressive;

▶ a number of visitors with appointments who cannot now be seen by the people with whom the appointments were made. (A variety of situations should be dealt with, for example, a person now has other commitments, a person is ill, someone else could offer to see the visitor).

▶ a visitor with an appointment who is now going to have to wait for a considerable time;

▶ a visitor who rushes in whilst you are dealing with someone else and wants your attention immediately because he is parked on a double-yellow line.

b) Check that you know your organisation's arrangements for the parking of visitors' cars.

c) Find out, if you do not already know, on whom you can call if you have a problem with a visitor, either through lack of knowledge or because the person is difficult in some way.

Reception Records

Visitors are frequently asked to sign a visitors' book or complete a visitor's card. Some organisations keep a reception register. This has the advantage not only of providing a permanent record of callers, but also shows who is on the premises in the event of an emergency, such as a fire. For this reason, people are often asked to sign out as well as in. Typically, the information required includes that shown in Figure 7.1, although the 'Reason for visit' and the 'To see' columns are not always included. A book which visitors must sign does have the disadvantage that callers can see who else is visiting the organisation. Badges, to be returned at the end of a visit, are sometimes given to visitors in order to identify those who are not members of staff.

Details of the most frequently used suppliers and of the most frequent visitors are often kept at the reception desk. This saves a great deal of time in looking up information for telephone use and avoids having to constantly ask visitors for their details. A card index is convenient for this purpose (see page 40).

Date: 15 August

Name	From	To see	Reason for visit	Apt	Time of arrival	Time of departure
J. Shanning	Suresales	Advertising Manager	To discuss advertising campaign	√	9.15	10.15
A. Singh	22 Green Rd Carnside	Mrs Jones	Interview for Wages Clerk vacancy	√	9.25	10.20
C. Prewitt	Mills & Co.	Buyer	Introduce new plastic material	×	9.30	asked to write in for an appointment
L. Hall	7 Brown St Carnside	Mrs Jones	Job interview	√	10.00	10.45
B. Brother	Office Supplies	Mr Grace	Demonstration of equipment	√	10.05	11.00
A. Wilson	Troublefree Ltd	Miss Simpson	To discuss new contract	√	10.15	11.15
J. Parkins	2 Victoria Ave Carnside	Mrs Jones	Interview for job	√	10.25	11.20
F. Calvi	Cardbox Ltd	Buyer	Special offer on packing materials	×	10.45	12.00

Figure 7.1 Reception register

Security of Information

The extent to which security of information is guarded will be determined by the work of the organisation. There are, therefore, variations in the degree of freedom within buildings that is allowed to visitors. In some organisations a commissionaire or someone on reception duty will escort visitors, but note that the reception desk must never be left unattended (see later). In organisations where security is less tight, visitors will be asked to make their own way to the office of the person expecting them. In others, that person's secretary or some other member of staff will go to reception to greet and escort visitors.

There will probably be occasions when you will be required to escort visitors. If so, engage the visitor in social pleasantries during the walk to the office. Make conversation regarding the visitor's journey, parking problems or that perennial favourite, the weather. Keep well away from discussion concerning the activities of the organisation or of any of its employees. It is not uncommon for staff to be actively 'pumped' by visitors for such information. The easiest way out if you ever find yourself in this situation is to simply plead ignorance of the matters under question.

You might need to formally introduce a visitor not previously known and should do so following the rules of introducing men to women, juniors to seniors and everyone to VIPs. Be sure to announce clearly the visitor's name, title and organisation. If the visitor is already known simply state, 'Mr Smith to see you.' Under no circumstances should you show anyone into an office unannounced or take a visitor to someone's office without first establishing that it is alright to do so.

Should you, on any occasion, have to leave someone alone by your own place of work it is wise to slip into a drawer or folder any documents which are lying around. A visitor, or indeed an unauthorised employee, should never have ready access to information which they might be able to use to commercial advantage or the detriment of a person. This includes a wider range of papers than those acknowledged as confidential, so it is best to be cautious.

Competence Builder 4   *(Elements 15.1, 15.2)*

In a real situation or in roleplay, deal with the following:

a) A visitor who has waited a long time and whom you now have to escort to your boss's office and introduce. He or she has not visited your organisation previously.

b) A visitor who tries to go somewhere unescorted or to some place where access is restricted.

c) A visitor who presses for information which cannot be disclosed.

d) A visitor who tries to avoid signing in.

MAINTAINING THE RECEPTION AREA

The reception area is usually situated near to the main entrance. Together with the image presented by the person on reception duty it plays a major role in determining the first impression a visitor forms of an organisation. If it is clean, bright, tidy and attractive the impression is likely to be favourable. The reverse is true if it is untidy and cluttered with personal belongings.

A reception area should have somewhere for people to sit whilst they are waiting and material to read. If visitors are sometimes offered a cup of tea or coffee then a table should be provided. Whether or not ash trays are provided depends upon the management's attitude towards smoking. A wastepaper basket, provided it is emptied regularly, is often a welcome addition. A coat stand is useful as people are often glad to get rid of bulky outdoor clothes, and somewhere secure where other belongings can be left is also appreciated.

Some reception areas are furnished lavishly. Some are used to publicise the work of the organisation through displays of products and wallcharts, and the provision of company literature.

Well-tended plants and flowers always help to make an area attractive. Fish tanks are sometimes used for the same purpose, as are pictures. Calendars and clocks can be both decorative and useful.

Amenities for which people pay are available in some reception areas, for example, pay phones and vending machines. In organisations, such as hotels, there are usually racks of items for sale, such as postcards and books.

Competence Builder 5   *(Element 15.2)*

Keep a notebook of places you visit in which to write down comments on their reception areas. If you do not normally visit many places where there are reception areas make a point of doing so. If, as a result of these visits, you can suggest improvements to the reception area of your own organisation do so to the appropriate person.

Security and Safety

▶ The reception area itself must be secure and never left unattended.

▶ Any cabinets, drawers etc. should be kept locked when not in use.

▶ If money is handled at reception, for any purpose, it must always be kept locked away when not needed and excess amounts removed at regular intervals.

▶ Windows and doors must be locked when the organisation is closed and these should be double-checked.

▶ If staff identity badges are in use they must be worn at all times.

▶ If visitors are issued with badges they should be asked to wear them where they can be seen.

▶ The reception register should be completed by everyone.

▶ The organisation's policy regarding whether or not visitors are escorted whilst on the premises must be followed at all times.

▶ If it is the organisation's policy that visitors' bags and briefcases are inspected this must be insisted upon even though it is sometimes a delicate request and task to carry out.

Competence Builder 6

(Elements 15.1, 15.2)

a) Constructively criticise the reception area of your organisation with regard to:
   ▶ safety;
   ▶ visitor comfort;
   ▶ enhancement, or otherwise, of the organisation's image.

b) In roleplay deal with:
   ▶ a visitor who asks for belongings to be stored safely;
   ▶ a visitor who is about to leave without his or her belongings.

c) In a real situation or realistic simulation carry out reception duties, such as receiving visitors, identifying their needs and directing/passing them on, as appropriate. Keep necessary records and maintain security and safety procedures. Arrange temporary cover as needed, in order to ensure that the reception is attended at all times. Maintain the reception area, ensuring that it is clean, tidy, bright and attractive, supplied with reading materials and with any notices kept up-to-date.

The Structure of the Organisation

In order to carry out reception duties efficiently it is necessary to know the structure of the organisation: briefly, what types of work are carried out in each section, and who works where and does what. This will enable you to know to whom visitors can be referred and where to find the members of staff that visitors ask for. You must also be familiar with your organisation's internal communication system(s).

Competence Builder 7   *(Elements 10.1, 14.1, 14.2, 15.1, 15.2, 19.2)*

a) Find out about your organisation. Draw up a chart/diagram to show the names/positions of people that visitors are likely to call to see. Include an outline of the main areas of work each deals with.

b) Check your knowledge of your organisation's internal communications system(s). Find out if there are internal directories or lists of internal telephone numbers. If there is a list of limited length then type a copy for yourself or make a photocopy. Consider if it would be appropriate to display this list in the reception area where it could be seen by visitors. If so, why? If not, why not?

c) Ask your boss or tutor to check your competence in using the internal communications system(s).

d) Discuss with a group of fellow trainees or students the importance of the image of the organisation, and the extent to which this can be enhanced or damaged by the reception area and those on duty in it.

Text Processing and Transcribing

If you are aiming for the Level II Business Administration (Secretarial) NVQ then you must prove your competence in the Text Processing Unit (for which you will be required to produce a variety of business documents from handwritten/type-written drafts), plus the Audio Transcription Unit or the Shorthand Transcription Unit (for which you will be required to produce a variety of business documents either from recorded speech or from dictated material).

The performance criteria which apply to all three units are as follows:

▶ The layout used must conform to the organisation's house style and/or accepted typing conventions. (In the absence of a house style accepted typing conventions are those laid down as the requirements of an approved examining and validating body.)

▶ Any corrections made are unobtrusive.

▶ All copies/originals/printouts are correctly collated and routed, as directed.

▶ The security and confidentiality of information is always maintained.

▶ Any equipment faults which arise are identified and reported promptly.

▶ Operating, safety and maintenance procedures are followed at all times.

In order to meet the competence requirements you must obviously be skilled in the use of your equipment and its care. For assessment purposes and, therefore, for practice, you can use any type of keyboarding equipment. Obviously, it enhances your skills if you are competent on a variety of keyboards and you should seize any opportunities that arise to practise on different ones.

You must also be able to proofread screen and printed documents efficiently because only then can you be sure of noticing any errors which you have made. Always check as you go along and, particularly if you are using a typewriter, check again before taking the paper out of the machine because of the difficulties of lining up. Remember that missing your own errors is a common occurrence. Get someone to work with you in checking anything complicated, with that person checking your work whilst you read from the original.

Competence Builder 1

(Elements 16.1, 17.1, 18.1 and where security and confidentiality of information must be maintained)

a) Obtain copies of non-confidential letters, memos, envelopes/labels, reports and any other documents which you might be required to type and for which your organisation has a standard layout. If it is more convenient, type-up mock documents. These need not be lengthy since the intention is that you use them as examples when setting out your own work.

b) Critically assess your own competence in making corrections. Practise, if necessary, until the corrections are, without question, unobtrusive.

c) Unless you already know, find out what the arrangements are in your organisation for ensuring that the security and confidentiality of information is always maintained.

d) Check the manual for keyboarding equipment that you use to ensure that you are fully aware of the operating, safety and maintenance procedures to be followed. Unless you already know to whom you should report any faults, find this out.

Proofreading on a screen is more difficult than proofreading a paper document and some errors, such as spacing faults, are easily missed. You might find that it helps to place your finger against the screen and move it along as you check each word, but this does mean that you have then to clean off any fingerprints and you could damage or mark delicate screens. It is also easy to miss small additions or deletions, and special instructions. So, if you are word processing, check that you have carried out all the functions required.

Competence Builder 2

(Elements 13.1, 13.2, 16.1, 17.1, 18.1)

a) Ask your boss or tutor to confirm that you are competent in checking your own work. If you are missing errors ask to be given additional proofreading work in order to practise this skill.

b) Check your knowledge of stationery sizes and qualities.

PRODUCING A VARIETY OF BUSINESS DOCUMENTS FROM HANDWRITTEN OR TYPEWRITTEN DRAFTS

The handwriting on some drafts sent for processing is not always clear, and what is written does not always make sense on first reading. It is usually time-saving to read quickly through the document to get the gist of it, marking any parts where the handwriting or meaning are not clear. You might have to refer to a dictionary or other reference book in order to check some words or verify these with the writer. If you process material on a regular basis for the same people then deciphering what has been written does become easier. You might have to rewrite some sections which are grammatically incorrect and refer to reference books in order to incorporate some information into the documents you are producing. If you are dealing with technical subject matters with which you are unfamiliar then you have to be particularly careful to ensure that what is produced is what is intended.

People usually require their work to be completed by a certain time so you must be able to plan and organise your work within deadlines, whilst at the same time allowing for any contingencies which often occur, such as being required to answer the telephone or deal with a fault on the equipment. There will undoubtedly also be occasions when you will be asked to deal with something particularly urgent. In this case, you might have to negotiate revised deadlines with your colleagues to give priority to the urgent work.

You should aim for competence in producing, letters, envelopes/labels, memos, reports, notices for display, tabulation, articles, and lists comprising alphabetical, numerical/chronological and general information. Your level of speed and accuracy should allow you to produce approximately 1200 words in a two and a half hour working period to a tolerance of no more than eight uncorrected spacing or typographical errors, with files (backup and/or hard copy) always produced and stored safely, and documents accurately amended as directed.

Competence Builder 3   *(Elements 16.1, 17.1, 18.1)*

a) Check the list of business documents stated as those which you must be competent in producing against a list of those which you normally deal with. Is there any category of documents which you are not currently required to produce? If so, ask your boss or tutor for opportunities to produce these.

b) Using your normal keyboarding equipment draw up a chart comparing type-writers and word processing equipment in such a way as to show clearly the benefits and limitations of each.

PRODUCING A VARIETY OF BUSINESS DOCUMENTS FROM RECORDED SPEECH

Some people who use audio equipment for dictation have been trained so as to use the facilities to the best advantage. They have, for example, been encouraged to speak clearly and at an even pace, to dictate instructions first in order to avoid unnecessary retyping, to use standard methods for indicating spelling, punctuation and paragraphing, and to be concise in what they dictate. Unfortunately, many dictators have not been trained and you must, therefore, expect recordings to be variable in quality, and to include interpolations and corrections.

Competence Builder 4

(Element 17.1)

Unless you have been trained and are competent to cope with 'office style' recorded dictation ask your boss or tutor if some less than perfect recordings can be provided for you to practise on.

In transcribing you must aim to produce approximately 600 words in a one and a half hour working period, to a tolerance of no more than four uncorrected spacing or typographical errors. The types of business documents you should expect to be able to produce from recorded speech are: short reports, letters, memos, notices for display and tabulation (involving text and figure work). You will only be considered competent if, when transcribing, you are also able to cope with interruptions, such as answering the telephone, deal with unforeseen machine problems, recognise when you must check something and rearrange your work-time in order to meet revised priorities.

Competence Builder 5

(Element 17.1)

Are you competent in producing from recorded speech all of the business documents stated? If not, ask for opportunities to produce those in which you still need practice.

Hints for Audio-Typewriting

▶ Make sure that you are thoroughly familiar with the equipment.

▶ Arrange your working space in a manner which will promote your efficiency, for example, keep reference books, stationery etc. close at hand.

▶ Check your headset or earpiece for comfort.

▶ Read or listen to any special instructions regarding layout, style, number of copies and order of priority.

▶ Note the indicated length of items to be transcribed and place the necessary stationery in order.

▶ Listen to the first few sentences of the dictation before starting to type if you are not familiar with the person's voice.

▶ Note any stated corrections to the dictation.

▶ Check any words which are not clear with the dictator or, if the person is not available, a colleague may be able to decipher them.

▶ Consult a dictionary for any spelling queries.

▶ Try to type continuously and listen intermittently. Do this by listening to as much of the text as you can carry in your head then commence typing. Before reaching the end listen to the next section. Aim to stop the machine as little as possible. You will be helped if the dictation is smooth, without breaks and at an appropriate speed.

▶ Check your work before passing it on, re-running the dictation if you have any doubts regarding accuracy or omissions.

PRODUCING A VARIETY OF BUSINESS DOCUMENTS FROM DICTATED MATERIAL

The obvious basic skill needed with dictation is a developed working knowledge and use of a shorthand system. You must be able to take shorthand notes at a minimum speed of 70 words per minute for competence at this level. These must be transcribed verbatim to produce approximately 375–400 words in a one hour working period, to a tolerance of no more than three uncorrected spacing or typographical errors. The production period is exclusive of dictation time. The types of business document you should expect to produce are letters, memos and short reports including some numerical data, such as dates, times and financial information. Naturally, you must expect to identify and check anything in the text about which you are uncertain, and rectify this.

Competence Builder 6   (Element 18.1)

a) Can you currently keep up a minimum speed of 70 words per minute for taking shorthand notes? Unless you can do so with 'office style' dictation get a fellow trainee, student or friend to dictate to you in this manner. Practise, practise, practise until you feel confident.

b) Can you meet the stated standard for transcription? If not, ask for and make opportunities for practice until you can.

c) Do you currently type the stated categories of business documents from your own shorthand notes? If not, ask for opportunities to do so.

Hints for Shorthand Dictation and Transcription

▶ Always take your notebook and pen/pencil with you whenever you might need to make notes or take a message. Do not keep your shorthand for formal dictation sessions.

▶ Always keep a well-sharpened pencil in reserve. Sharpen your pencils at both ends unless it is inconvenient to carry them like this.

▶ Date each page – at the bottom is often the most convenient place if you need to refer back later.

- ▶ Keep a rubber band around used pages to save having to search for the next fresh page.
- ▶ Rule a narrow margin (left side for right-handed people, right for left-handed) for notes and minor corrections.
- ▶ Adopt your own standard system for long corrections or additions, for example, asterisks or footnotes.
- ▶ Concentrate on the dictation, firmly avoiding any distractions.
- ▶ If the dictation is too fast then say so. The dictator will prefer to slow down rather than be given incorrect documents.
- ▶ Punctuate the shorthand as much as possible when actually writing it – definitely inserting full stops and new paragraphs where apparent. This will be largely determined by the dictator's style.
- ▶ Always make sure that you have the addressee's correct name, and address where appropriate, either dictated or from a document.
- ▶ Adopt a system for indicating priorities, otherwise transcribe your notes in order of dictation. It is worth asking the dictator, when the dictation is finished, if there are any urgent items.
- ▶ Draw a line across the page after the dictation for each item.
- ▶ Do not interrupt the dictation if you have a query. Make a note in the margin and ask your question at the end of the dictation for that item.
- ▶ If the time is interrupted use the time to check that what you have taken down so far is clear to you.
- ▶ If the interruption is in the form of a telephone call or someone wishes to speak to the dictator, try to establish, using appropriate gestures, whether you should leave the room.
- ▶ Before commencing to type each item read through your notes on it to ensure that it makes sense, that you are aware of any special instructions, and to give yourself an opportunity to raise any necessary queries or obtain any reference material needed.
- ▶ Mark the place you have reached in your notes, should an interruption occur when you are transcribing.
- ▶ Cross through each item when transcribed.
- ▶ Write on the front of each notebook the dates of commencement and finish, and file them in chronological order. If you have more than one clearly-defined area of work it might be worth considering using a separate notebook for each, but take care not to make this a complicated arrangement.

Competence Builder 7 *(Element 18.1)*

Use shorthand whenever you can, for making notes, taking messages and for personal use. Work towards it being as natural for you to write in shorthand as it is in longhand.

English Skills

Unfortunately, it is not always recognised by aspiring secretaries that shorthand, typing, audio-typing and word processing skills, no matter how good, are insufficient in themselves. In order to transcribe shorthand and audio material, and produce typed copy from handwritten and typed drafts, you must be able to spell and punctuate correctly.

Spelling is a problem for many people, but one which you cannot afford to have. A dictionary is useful, but only when you know that you are uncertain of a spelling. Read for pleasure and practise the spelling of words that you know you find difficult. Electronic typewriters and word processors with spelling-check programs are available, but cannot be relied on as standard issue. It would not go down well at an interview if you asked, 'Does the typewriter I'll be using have a built-in spelling checker?'

Competence Builder 8

(Elements 12.2, 14.3, 16.1, 17.1, 18.1 and throughout)

Critically assess your ability to spell, punctuate and use grammar correctly and efficiently. If you make mistakes or have particular difficulties, do you recognise them? If not, get someone to look over your work and help you to become aware of errors. This is an important first step and one you must take before really beginning to progress. Practise anything which is a problem until it ceases to be so.

Arranging Travel and Booking Accommodation

Many business people are required to travel in connection with their work, for example, to attend meetings and conferences, and visit business contacts. Making the travel arrangements and booking any accommodation are business admini-stration tasks with which you must be familiar.

MAKING TRAVEL ARRANGEMENTS

Attention to detail in making these arrangements is essential. This applies equally to local visits and those to far-distant places. Things can go wrong, but this must never be as a result of your work. The basic planning routine is always the same regardless of destination, so you can work confidently with a common checklist.

The arrangements made must reflect the travellers' requirements, so these have to be established first. Find out where the visit is to, for how long and any preferred means of travel. The next thing to do is to open a file for holding all the papers connected with the trip, such as items to do with travel, insurance and accommodation. A tick-off checklist of matters to be attended to, especially with space for adding notes, is invaluable. For convenience, this can be written inside the front cover of the file. If you have to arrange frequent trips it is worthwhile keeping a supply of checklists so that a copy is always available for fastening inside the cover of each file, immediately it is opened. If the checklist is comprehensive enough for the most complicated visits then unnecessary items can be crossed off when less detailed arrangements are required. This guards against the danger of omitting some detail when a job appears to be simple.

Competence Builder 1
(Element 19.1)

Start a checklist of items that you think would have to be attended to when making arrangements for a business trip. Make additions as your work on this unit helps to increase your awareness of what is involved.

It is important not to make the travel arrangements too tight on time as there can be delays, especially if the traveller has to fit in with other people's plans. This will need to be discussed with the person for whom the arrangements are being made or, where appropriate, with the secretary who is making appointments connected with the visit. Public and religious holidays should also be borne in mind, for both departure and arrival locations, as transport is often minimal at such times. This should be thought about particularly when making arrangements for overseas visits where public holidays are on different dates from our own.

Some large firms have their own travel service departments which make reservations, book accommodation, obtain travel documents and generally give advice. If you work in such an organisation, all you will probably need to do is give that department the basic information and the rest will be done. This has the advantage of saving time and of being able to draw upon the expertise, knowledge and contacts of specialist staff. You should, however, still aim to be competent in making travel arrangements yourself so that you could do so in an emergency, or if you worked in future in an organisation without such facilities.

Some firms have an account with a travel agency which they use as required. In addition to booking passages and flights, a number of agencies will assist with documents, insurance matters, accommodation, the hiring of cars and other services, such as secretarial and interpreting, needed by business people. This expert attention is helpful, but when you have been given the job of making the arrangements, the final responsiblity for checking that all has been dealt with is yours.

For those who have to deal with all the arrangements themselves, there are a number of sources of reference including AA and RAC handbooks, British Rail timetables and various hotel guides. High street travel agencies can, of course, be used on an *ad hoc* basis, and are often the quickest and most convenient source of reference and service.

Competence Builder 2   *(Element 19.1)*

a) Are any outside agencies used by your organisation for making travel arrangements? If so, find out what services they currently provide. What other services could they offer and at what cost?

b) Draw up a list of reference books and other sources of information for arranging travel, both in this country and abroad.

Itineraries

An itinerary is a combined programme and timetable. It shows the times and nature of engagements, people to be met, travel and other details (see Figure 9.1). Drafting a skeleton itinerary is a good way to begin the actual planning, since it provides a framework into which you can slot the various arrangements as they are made. When all have been settled, you can type up the final version. The form this takes will depend on the length and type of visit, but should be convenient for reference. A separate card or sheet for each day is useful; so is a mini-version for slipping into a pocket or bag.

```
ITINERARY - TUESDAY 6 JUNE 19—

09.30    Depart Kings Cross
10.40    Arrive Peterborough (car from No.2 Branch)
11.00    Preliminary Briefing No.2 Branch Manager
         (Mr. Robinson)
11.30    Meeting of Peterborough Sales Staff - plans
         for launch of 'Zippyclens'
12.30    Lunch with Mr. Robinson and assistant
         (Miss Barrowcliffe)
13.45    Car to Stamford No.3 Branch
14.30    Preliminary Briefing No.3 Branch Manger
         (Mr. Wilkinson)
15.00    Meeting Stamford Sales Staff - plans for
         launch of 'Zippyclens'
         Retirement presentation to Miss Snow
16.45    Car to Peterborough station
17.36    Depart Peterborough (refreshment facilities)
18.43    Arrive Kings Cross
```

Figure 9.1 Itinerary

Means of Travel

Travelling takes time, often a considerable amount, but depending upon the mode of travel this time can gainfully be used for working, eating or resting.

Rail travel, without a change en route, is generally quick and allows the optimum use of time for reading, writing and thinking through recent events or forthcoming engagements. A wise precaution is to book a seat for the traveller, especially if the train is a popular one at a busy time, if the traveller has a preference for sitting face or back to the engine, or wishes to be in a smoking or non-smoking section. If a train has a restaurant car, time can be saved by lunching or dining in it. In any event it is necessary to find out whether or not a buffet facility is available, since provision for at least light refreshments should be made. If the train journey is a long one then travelling at night, with a booked sleeping compartment, is a good option.

Air travel is the quickest once the traveller is airborne, but time in getting to and from an airport, and the time that must be allowed for checking-in and baggage reclaim, can considerably increase the time allowed for the journey.

When a car is needed during a trip, it is often decided that a hired vehicle will be picked up from the station or airport since this is less tiring than driving the whole distance and might be quicker. If you have to book a car check that the driver can meet any conditions made, such as being over a certain age and having held a valid licence for a stated period. Remember to make arrangements for the car to be garaged either at the hotels or at local garages. Always check parking facilities at any location to be visited and remember also to include 'parking' on the checklist.

Competence Builder 3   *(Element 19.1)*

a) Decide, and then check your suggestions with your boss or tutor, the means of travel you would be likely to have to arrange for a colleague who wishes to:

   i) Visit two firms in the centre of London.
   ii) Visit a town 80 miles away with a stopover for a meeting on the way.
   iii) Attend a whole day meeting in Glasgow. (Assume your organisation is in London and your colleague can only be away from work on the day of the meeting.)

b) What arrangements would you have to make in each case? From where and how would you find out the information which will allow you to make these?

Travel Abroad

When making arrangements for travel abroad, you will need information about the documents required, acceptable methods of payment and how to obtain hard cash for each country being visited.

Travellers require a valid full passport, obtainable from a passport office either in person or by post, or a British Visitor's Passport. The latter has the advantage of being obtainable immediately from a main post office, but it is only valid for one year (a full passport is valid for ten years), and its acceptance is limited to certain countries. Some countries require a visa and these can take time to obtain.

Proof of smallpox vaccination and various innoculations is required for travel to certain countries. These regulations must be ascertained well in advance, to allow for innoculations to be obtained and for any necessary time for the innoculations to become effective.

You also need to obtain insurance cover – personal, baggage and health. In connection with the latter, there is some cover available under reciprocal arrangements between EC countries but this is by no means as comprehensive as that which is available in Britain. If travel is to be by car then additional documents are required – motoring organisations such as the AA and the RAC can advise on this.

The Department of Trade and Industry (DTI) publish a series of booklets entitled *Hints to Exporters*. These cover different countries and contain information on passport, visa and health regulations; currency and exchange control regulations; area, population, and principal towns and cities; travel routes, hotels and restaurants; postal, telephone and telegraphic facilities; climate, clothing and hours of business; and other useful details for business and travel. The booklets can be obtained from DTI regional offices or the London head office.

Competence Builder 4

(Element 19.1)

a) For which countries is a visa required?

b) Obtain details of the medical attention that one can receive under reciprocal EC agreements.

c) List the countries which have medical requirements, such as proof of inoculations, and state what these requirements are.

d) Obtain information regarding the various insurance policies available for travellers.

e) Find out about international time zones. How could these affect:

▶ your work in making arrangements for visits?

▶ the traveller?

Taking Money Abroad

Banks will supply information regarding the various means available for taking money out of the country and obtaining cash abroad. There are a number of alternatives, each has advantages and disadvantages with regard to safety, overall convenience, cost, and how quickly and easily hard cash can be obtained.

Competence Builder 5

(Element 19.1)

a) Obtain information as to the alternative means available for taking money abroad. Where available, collect leaflets for reference.

b) Can currency be obtained for all countries? Is it necessary to give notice when either travellers' cheques or currency is required?

c) Find out to which countries people in your organisation travel for business purposes. Using a calculator work out for each of these countries the amount of foreign currency that you would receive for £117.36. If people do not travel for business in your organisation then do your calculations based on the EC countries.

BOOKING ACCOMMODATION

It is necessary to discuss the location of any hotels being booked with the person requiring the accommodation, since it is important to bear in mind the appointments to be kept and the means of travel to be used. When making arrangements, remember also that convenient and comfortable accommodation is important on a business trip. Special requirements regarding diet, availability of a meal upon arrival, type of room and possibly facilities for the entertaining of guests, have to be determined and arranged for. All bookings, special requests and instructions should, without exception, be confirmed in writing.

Competence Builder 6

(Element 19.1)

In a real situation or realistic simulation make the arrangements for colleagues who have to take business trips on at least four separate occasions. Each occasion should require accommodation to be booked and at least one trip should be overseas. Your plans should accurately reflect the stated requirements and be consistent with your organisation's policy. Therefore you will need to find out and use laid-down booking procedures and be aware of any structure of allowances. You should also check if your organisation has a list of preferred hotels, but should in every case consult a hotel guide in order to be able to offer an alternative, if needed.

a) In each case, plan the travel arrangements and offer, where appropriate, alternative methods of travel. Estimate the distance, state the time involved and work out costs. Provide instructions and maps as appropriate.

b) In the case of overseas visits, determine the amount of funds required, both in travellers' cheques and currency, and provide the traveller with information on how to obtain these, together with the cost. Calculate the amount of foreign currency that can currently be obtained per £100. Check passport, visa and vaccination requirements, as appropriate.

c) Find appropriate accommodation and type/draft letters to the hotels confirming arrangements you have made by telephone. If necessary in simulation, ask on at least one occasion for a specifically-located room and make a special dietary request.

d) Keep a record of all arrangements made and present these in a convenient form in good time to the travellers, together with any necessary documents.

Arranging Meetings

Meetings take place at all levels, from board meetings at the top to meetings involving junior members of staff. They offer an opportunity for matters and suggestions to be discussed, opinions to be put forward and decisions made. They provide a neutral ground to discuss conflicting opinions and, by a process of talking through the issues, allow for differences to be resolved.

DOCUMENTATION

Meetings can be informal or formal. If the latter, then they are conducted by the chairperson according to laid-down rules of conduct. Other rules ensure that everyone entitled to attend is invited to do so and that they receive the necessary documents.

The responsibility for this documentation and the organisation of regular formal meetings is usually that of an appointed meetings' secretary. Since a great deal of work is frequently required some of this may be delegated to administrative staff. Such staff can also be involved when meetings are less formal or irregular and the appointment of a meetings' secretary is not warranted. The arranging of meetings thus becomes a task which anyone in business administration might be called upon to perform. It is one in which those working along the administrative and secretarial routes towards the Level II Business Administration NVQ are required to prove competence.

Notice of Meeting

All those who have a right to be present at a formal meeting must be notified in writing that a meeting has been called. The notice must be sent out a minimum period in advance, and state clearly the type of meeting, the day and date, time and place where it is to be held. This minimum period excludes the day of posting and the day of the meeting. It is laid down in the standing orders which set out the rules of the organisation. In some instances, it is acceptable for the notice of a meeting to be displayed in a prominent place.

Select any two meetings which take place regularly in your organisation, prefer-ably of different types, for example, one involving staff only and one which exter-nal people attend.

a) Find out the dates of the next meetings and any rules which apply regarding the period of notice. On what dates will these need to be sent out to fulfil the minimum notice period requirements?

b) Type or write out the notices of meeting using the 24-hour clock.

Agenda

This is the programme of business to be discussed at the meeting with each item listed in the order in which it will be taken. It usually incorporates the notice calling the meeting. It is drawn up, in consultation with the chairperson, using information from various sources. It might include matters which have recently arisen, those held over from a previous meeting and items suggested by members. Since the agenda provides an opportunity for members to think in advance about the business to be discussed, the more clearly it is worded the more fruitfully it can be used.

There are certain items common to most agendas, starting with the announcing of apologies from those absent. This is followed by the acceptance of the minutes of the previous meeting and a consideration of matters arising from them. Any correspondence which has been received is then dealt with, followed by the main items of business. If these are arranged in order of importance this allows less important matters to be left to a future meeting, should time run out.

The item 'any other business', commonly abbreviated to AOB, gives members an opportunity to bring up matters which have arisen since the agenda was compiled. It must be confined, however, to minor items since members will not have had prior notice of the topics and those absent will not have had an opportunity to make their opinions known. Examples of acceptable 'any other business' are an expression of thanks for work done or a decision to send flowers to someone who is ill. This item appears before the final one of date, time and place (if it varies) for the next meeting. An example of a standard type of agenda is shown in Figure 10.1

A sufficient number of copies of the agenda should be produced to allow for an additional copy to be given to those who omit to bring theirs with them to the meeting. As this is a common occurrence, it might be a matter of policy to place automatically a copy before each seat at the meeting. This does not actually waste paper, copies have to be available anyway, and it does save time and embarrassment.

Millingfield Writers' Group

NOTICE OF MEETING

6 February 19—

A meeting of the committee will be held in the library resource room at Millingfield College on Wednesday 14 February 19— commencing at 19.00 hours.

AGENDA

1. Apologies for absence

2. Minutes of the last meeting

3. Matters arising

4. Correspondence

5. Plans for Poetry Reading Evening 15 March 19—

6. Future members' evenings – please bring ideas

7. Feasibility of purchasing a copier to be considered

8. Any other business

9. Date, time and place of next meeting

M. ROBINSON
Hon. Secretary

Figure 10.1 Notice of meeting and agenda for a committee meeting

Competence Builder 2   (Element 19.2)

Compile agendas for the meetings selected for Competence Builder 1. If necessary, ask for help from those who normally prepare them. If possible, carry out this task under real conditions and reproduce, by suitable means, the number of copies required. At all times, remember to maintain the security and confidentiality of the information with which you are dealing.

The Minutes

Minutes are a concise record of the business discussed and the decisions made at a meeting. Since the agenda is the programme, the order of the items on it will be repeated in the minutes. Minutes are 'approved' by members at the following meeting. Sometimes they are actually read out. The chairperson then asks those who were present at the meeting if what has been recorded is a true record. If all agree, the chairperson will sign the minutes to indicate this.

It is quite common, and less time-consuming, for copies of the minutes to be circulated prior to the meeting at which they are to be approved. The chairperson will then ask if they can be taken 'as read'. If agreed the minutes will then be signed without being read out.

FACILITIES

In addition to ensuring that meeting documents are prepared and distributed, a room must be booked, plus at least light refreshments, for example, coffee and biscuits, and visual aids, such as a flipchart or overhead projector if required. Doing this on the telephone is convenient because it allows for discussion, is speedy, and you know immediately if the facilities required are available. All arrangements made must be confirmed in writing.

Competence Builder 3   *(Element 19.2)*

Find out with whom catering arrangements for a meeting can be made, both inside the organisation and with local agencies. What are the names of the people with whom you would have to liaise? In both cases, find out what could be offered (drink and biscuits/finger buffet/full meal), the costs and if there is sufficient choice to cater, for example, for vegetarians.

Visual Aids

It is becoming increasingly common for visual aids to be used during meetings and you should make a point of becoming familiar with the various aids that might be used and from where these might be obtained. They could be available in the organisation, particularly if it has a training department, but can also be hired. Having this information to hand could prove invaluable should an occasion arise when you are required to obtain such equipment quickly.

Competence Builder 4   *(Element 19.2)*

a) Find out from where the following aids can be obtained either within your own organisation or externally: video recorder, television receiver, tape recorder, overhead projector and screen, whiteboard/flipchart and stand.

b) How much would each cost to hire, by the day, if it is necessary to obtain them externally?

c) If any of these aids are available within the organisation:
   ▶ find out how they work;
   ▶ find out what could go wrong and how to deal with it, for example if the overhead projector bulb does not come on or goes out during use.

Additional Duties

People are sometimes invited to address meetings on matters upon which they can give specialist opinion or advice. It might fall on you to have to liaise with them and make whatever arrangements are necessary. These could include travel information and bookings, accommodation and meal reservations.

Another task is the providing of directions and maps for those attending a meeting who are unfamiliar with the venue. There must be no slip-up here. Make sure that maps are copied from a reliable source and try the directions out on someone who can be relied on to give constructive criticism.

Competence Builder 5

(Element 19.2)

Prepare maps and directions suitable for sending to an external person who has to attend, for the first time, a meeting in your organisation:

a) From the nearest main highway or motorway. Advise them on arrangements for parking when they arrive.

b) From the train station.

In both cases, either get someone to try out your maps and directions, or ask a colleague for constructive criticism.

PLANNING

In order to ensure that no job is missed it is a good plan to work with a checklist. This can be conveniently divided up into jobs to do in advance and jobs to do on the day of the meeting.

Jobs to Do in Advance

▶ If required to do so, check that participants have been informed of arrangements and will be available.

▶ Check that the room to be used is available and book it. Confirm this in writing.

▶ Note in any diaries for which you are responsible the date, time, place and nature of the meeting.

▶ Arrange for the preparation and reproduction of meeting papers as directed.

▶ Send out all necessary papers/letters of confirmation as directed.

▶ Book any necessary visual aids and confirm by memo (internal) or letter (external).

▶ Order refreshments or make catering arrangements as required, and confirm by memo or letter.

Jobs to Do on the Day of the Meeting

▶ If needed, arrange for direction signs to the meeting room to be displayed and inform the receptionist as to where people should be directed.

▶ Place a notice on the door stating 'Meeting in progress'.

▶ Check the room for:
ventilation;
heating;
adequate seating;
availability of water and glasses, and ashtrays placed on the table if smoking is permitted;
'No smoking' signs, if appropriate;
name cards, if used. These can be either placed on the table or, if members are free to choose their own seats, left near the door to be picked up.

▶ Date the page of the attendance register and place it ready for the chairperson to sign, prior to signing by the rest of those attending.

▶ Place spare copies of the agenda, the minutes of the last meeting, paper, pencils and pens, on a table just inside the door or somewhere convenient, for anyone who might have forgotten theirs.

▶ Check that any visual aids ordered have been delivered and are working.

▶ Make a last-minute check and confirm times for refreshments with both the caterer and the chairperson.

▶ If required assist visitors as they arrive, taking coats etc. and/or serve refreshments.

▶ After the meeting, check the room to ensure that nothing has been left and, if appropriate, any visual aids used have been collected.

Competence Builder 6

(Element 19.2)

1. In a real situation or realistic simulation, arrange a meeting on two separate occasions involving three or more people. One meeting should be internal, one external and each should include at least one external participant. Both should require the provision of refreshments and a visual aid. In each case carry out the following activities using the 24-hour clock:

   a) Check the availability of the participants and the facilities required against the proposed meeting date(s) and agree a definite date and time.

   b) Make, and confirm in writing, arrangements for the meeting room, refreshments and visual aids.

   c) Advise the participants of the arrangements and, for at least one of the meetings, send all necessary papers to them in advance.

2. If not currently involved with the arrangements for meetings, liaise with a colleague who is so involved in order to arrange to 'shadow' that person when a check is being made that all is ready on the day of a meeting. Afterwards, refer to the jobs to do shown above and type or write out a checklist adapted to your circumstances. Is there anything else you would have done had you been responsible for the arrangements?

Processing Payments

The extent to which you are, at any one time, involved in the various aspects of processing payments depends upon the organisation you work for and the position you hold. You might, therefore, be called upon to carry out some or all of the tasks dealt with in this unit. For example, you may have to look after the petty cash, receive and record payments and issue receipts for them, carry out routine banking transactions, and make payments to suppliers and others. Whatever your role, you must always handle cash in a manner which ensures its security, complete any necessary forms and records without error, and produce accurate financial calculations (for which task you will be expected to use a calculator efficiently).

The tasks cited in this unit are common ones, but the procedures for carrying them out do vary. In order to ensure that you follow those laid down by your organisation you should, when undertaking new duties, check through with someone familiar with the tasks exactly what it is that you are going to do.

MAKING AND RECORDING PETTY CASH PAYMENTS

Small incidental business expenses paid in cash are usually accounted for by means of a petty cash system. The items commonly dealt with in this manner include telephone calls made from outside the office, bus fares incurred in the course of business, cleaning materials, postage stamps, magazines and flowers.

Since an organisation's main cashier is usually a senior member of staff carrying a major responsiblity, it is inappropriate for this person to be dealing with minor cash payments. These are generally made, therefore, by a more junior member of staff from a petty cash float kept on an imprest system. This system is a carefully-controlled one which allows for a check to be made at any time to ensure that the records are precise and accurate, and that there is no money deficit through accidental loss or pilfering. You may well find yourself in the role of petty cashier at some time in your working life, and if so one of the most important things you must ensure is that the cash is protected against theft.

Security of Cash

The cash must be kept in a locked box which in turn is locked away in a safe, cupboard or drawer. When the box is in use do not place it where others can easily access it.

As the person responsible for the petty cash you should:

▶ Keep the keys to the box, and the cupboard or drawer where it is kept.

▶ Have an arrangement for someone to deputise in the event of your absence so that petty cash requests can continue to be dealt with. Whatever the arrangements, limit access to the keys.

▶ Never leave cash lying around, no matter how little there is of it or for how short a period of time.

▶ Count any change to be given and hand it over before the money tendered is put away. The mistake of giving change for a different value note cannot then be made, neither can anyone falsely claim this to be so.

▶ Keep accurate and up-to-date records of all monies, in and out.

▶ Doubly-check the forms used and the cash movements against them, to make sure that they match.

▶ Count money out in front of, and pay it directly to, the person claiming it, in order to avoid any later claims of error.

▶ Never mix petty cash and personal money whether this may be for the purpose of providing sufficient 'change' or a temporary borrowing. This can lead to error and charges of dishonesty, however innocent your intention.

Competence Builder 1

(Element 20.1)

What security rules apply in your organisation to ensure safety of the petty cash. Can you suggest any measures which could tighten-up existing security?

Imprest System

The imprest, or float, kept for petty cash is usually part of the organisation's main cash balance. The amount for petty cash is usually sufficient to cover payments for a given period of time, say a week or a month. If there appears to be a change in demand for petty cash, which is likely to continue, then the imprest amount is adjusted.

Each time money is required from petty cash you hand this out in return for a petty cash voucher stating the amount. This means that your cash-in-hand plus the total of the vouchers always adds up to the full amount of the imprest.

You keep a petty cash account and balance it at the end of the stated period. You then take this with the vouchers and the petty cash float to the main cashier. This person, after checking, will then give you a sum of money equal to the stated expenditure which will restore the float to the full amount again.

Petty Cash Vouchers

These are numbered for precise identification. On them is written the date, what the cash is to be spent on and the amount required. Pads of pre-printed forms are generally used; some have a VAT column, but many do not since the sums involved are small and not thought to be worth accounting for separately.

A voucher is used every time a payment has to be made, or an item purchased, from petty cash money. The voucher is completed and signed by the person requiring the money. It should always be countersigned by a senior person empowered to authorise the expenditure (see Figure 11.1).

Sometimes an item is purchased prior to obtaining petty cash for it. In this case the person making the purchase obtains a receipt and hands it in with a petty cash voucher as a claim for a refund of the money spent.

Petty Cash Voucher	Folio _CB2/89_ Date _20 Feb_ 19–	
For what required	AMOUNT	
Stationery	5	66
VAT		99
	6	65
Signature _S. Higgins_		
Passed by _G. M. Needham_		

Figure 11.1 Petty cash voucher

Cash-in-Hand Vouchers

One reason for making a purchase prior to obtaining the petty cash is that the price of the item is not known. This can be covered by the use of a cash-in-hand voucher. A standard petty cash voucher is completed with a note added 'cash-in-hand'. Stated on the voucher is a sum of money expected to be sufficient to cover the purchase and this is the amount of cash you pay out. After the purchase, a further voucher is filled in for the exact amount. When this is presented you make a cash adjustment and destroy the cash-in-hand voucher.

You do need to be vigilant in order to avoid error when handling cash-in-hand vouchers because of the possibility of items being authorised twice. With care, however, this should not arise and cash-in-hand vouchers overcome the problem of someone having to make a payment when they have not got spare personal cash. The rule that every penny taken out of petty cash has to be supported by a voucher is maintained and it is a convenient variation on the system for occasional use.

Always ask for receipts when cash-in-hand vouchers have been used. These are attached to the relevant petty cash vouchers which are filed after being entered in the petty cash book.

You can make a check of the petty cash at any time by adding the amounts on the vouchers together and subtracting this from the total amount of the petty cash float. The difference should equal the amount of cash in the petty cash box.

Competence Builder 2   *(Element 20.1)*

a) As the petty cashier what would cause you to ask questions or refuse to make payments when requested?

b) How would you file petty cash vouchers? Why?

Petty Cash Book

This is similar to the main cash book and contains the petty cash account. It is, therefore, part of the double-entry system. The amounts given to you for your float are credited in the main cash book and debited in the petty cash book. Petty cash expenditure is credited in the petty cash book and debited in the appropriate ledger accounts.

Petty cash amounts are relatively small, can be numerous and for a variety of items. Posting these individually to the nominal ledger accounts would, therefore, be time-consuming and lead to a profusion of entries in these accounts. In order to avoid this, an analysed petty cash book is used. This allows for the posting of periodic totals for each type of expenditure to the ledger accounts.

The petty cash account shows the amount of cash received for the petty cash float with the main cash book folio against it and the date. The items for which payment has been made are entered, plus the voucher numbers and the total cash paid for each. These amounts are then entered again in the appropriate analysis columns which are headed in accordance with each main class of expenditure, for example, postage, cleaning, office sundries, travel, and when appropriate VAT (see Figure 11.2).

Dr. **Cr.**

PETTY CASH ACCOUNT

| CASH RECEIVED | | | CASH PAID | | | | ANALYSIS | | | | |
Date	Folio	Amount	Date	Details	Voucher No.	Amount Paid	Stationery	Postage	Travel	Office Expenses	VAT
Feb 1	CB2	7 21		Balance b/d							
		42 79		Cash received							
			Feb 2	Cleaning windows	82	11 75				10 00	1 75
			„ 5	Flower vase	83	3 05				2 60	45
			„ 7	Envelopes	84	4 38	3 73				65
			„ 9	Postage	85	6 60		6 60			
			„ 13	Fares	86	1 22			1 22		
			„ 14	Coffee	87	1 87				1 87	
			„ 16	Milk	88	3 00				3 00	
			„ 20	Stationery – miscellaneous	89	6 65	5 66				99
			„ 21	Biscuits	90	48				48	
			„ 23	Postage	91	2 45		2 45			
			„ 28	Fares	92	76			76		
						42 21	9 39	9 05	1 98	17 95	3 84
			„ 28	Balance c/d		7 79					
		50 00				50 00					
Mar 1	CB3	7 79		Balance b/d							
		42 21		Cash received							

Figure 11.2 Petty cash account

The use of analysis columns means that each class of expenditure can be totalled separately at the end of the petty cash period. Each column represents an account in the ledger to which the totals can be readily transferred. In addition to totalling the columns the account is balanced to show the amount of imprest still held.

Competence Builder 3

(Elements 20.1, 23.1)

a) There are two checks which should automatically follow the totalling of the analysis columns and the balancing of the account. What are they? Discuss the importance of these checks with your boss or tutor and suggest what you would do if there are discrepancies.

b) Make notes which indicate that you:
   i) understand the benefits of the imprest system;
   ii) understand the relationship between petty cash records and other accounts records. If necessary, talk to people responsible for these records.

Show your notes to your boss or tutor in order to check your understanding.

You should enter the petty cash vouchers into the petty cash account at regular intervals. The frequency of this might be laid down by your organisation. Even if it is not, it is nevertheless best to complete this task frequently so that it does not become too time-consuming on any one occasion. You will also find that keeping the account up-to-date lessens the possibility of error.

Should you find what appears to be a discrepancy in cash, or an error in the records you must investigate and try to resolve this immediately. If you are not able to do so then the matter should be reported to a more senior person.

In handling petty cash records you must always follow the procedures laid down by your organisation in regard to financial matters.

Competence Builder 4

(Element 20.1)

In a real situation or realistic simulation, carry out petty cash procedures ensuring that:

▶ All transactions are accurately recorded and supported by correctly authorised petty cash vouchers.

▶ Cash withdrawals from the main cash account are accurately recorded.

▶ All queries are investigated and promptly referred or resolved.

▶ Cash handling security and safety procedures are always followed.

▶ Cash and petty cash book records are accurately balanced, as directed.

▶ Confidentiality procedures are always followed.

Value Added Tax (VAT)

Value added tax (VAT) might or might not have to be dealt with as part of your duties as petty cashier. This is because VAT is not paid on everything, including a number of items for which petty cash is commonly used. The total VAT for this account can thus be quite small and some organisations do not consider it worth the additional work involved in claiming back the VAT on these items.

When, however, it is the policy of an organisation to claim back the VAT paid on petty cash items, then an analysis column for VAT needs to be added to the account. The VAT paid is stated in this and then deducted from the total for the item. These balances are then placed in the analysis columns according to the expenditure category (see Figure 11.2).

VAT is also discussed in Unit 14, on page 136.

Competence Builder 5 *(Element 20.1)*

If not already known, find out the guidelines in your organisation regarding the handling of VAT in the petty cash account.

RECEIVING AND RECORDING PAYMENTS AND ISSUING RECEIPTS

You should expect to handle payments in cash, by cheque or by credit card, and must aim to become familiar quickly with the documentation for these. You need also to be knowledgeable about different methods of payment and the implication of their use.

Payment by Cash

Payments in cash are simple in that there are no documents connected with the actual method of payment. You have, of course, to be particularly careful not to make mistakes in counting cash and giving change, and should learn techniques for handling it efficiently. You must also ensure that cash is secure at all times, and must learn to operate a till or cash drawer, some of which are easy but others are not.

The preparation and issuing of receipts, and the completion of any records required are common to all payment methods. You have also to balance the total cash taken against the record of takings – usually at the end of the day – and when doing this should remember to deduct the float of change with which you normally start the day.

Competence Builder 6 *(Elements 20.1, 20.2, 20.3, 22.2)*

How are cash payments dealt with in your organisation? Notice how people count money and handle change, for example, how bank clerks count notes. Practise this and similar techniques until you become a skilled handler of cash.

Payment by Cheque

The first essential in receiving a payment by cheque is to confirm the validity of the presented cheque. You need, therefore, to know what appears on it, what you can accept, that the payee is the person to whom the cheque is made payable and the drawer is the account holder.

There are several numbers on a cheque. Along the bottom is shown, in magnetic characters, the cheque number, the sorting code of the bank branch holding the drawer's current account (which is repeated in the top right corner), and the drawer's account number.

The appropriate spaces on a cheque offered in payment are filled in and it is signed by the drawer. If a mistake has been made it is acceptable for this to be altered, provided the drawer's signature is added to the alteration. You should not accept an altered cheque without this addition.

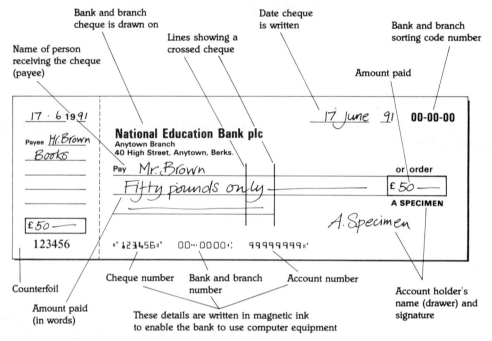

Figure 11.3 Crossed cheque and counterfoil

Crossed cheques have two parallel lines across the face of the cheque (see Figure 11.3). They are in common use and are safer than uncrossed cheques because they have to be paid into a bank account. They are thus less open to misuse by an unauthorised person.

Post-dated cheques are ones which are dated ahead. Unless specifically instructed to do so, these should not be accepted because the bank will not process them until the date shown. Stale cheques, as the name indicates, are old ones. Payment will not usually be made by a bank on cheques which are more than six months old.

Upon receiving a cheque you must look to see that it has been made out correctly in every detail, and note particularly that the words and figures stating the amount of money agree.

The drawer can request his bank to stop payment of a cheque, but not if the cheque is guaranteed by a cheque card, and payment was made in accordance with conditions governing the use of these.

Cheque cards

Cheque cards guarantee payment of cheques up to the limit stated on the card and you can confidently accept payment by this means. Note that the amount stated is the limit up to which each transaction paid for by cheque is guaranteed. You must not, therefore, accept two cheques each made out for £50 in payment for one transaction of £100, if the customer's cheque card has a £50 limit.

Included on the cards is the sorting code of the bank branch holding the cheque drawer's current account, the card number and the date of its expiry. In addition, the account holder's name appears and the card has to be signed by this person.

A cheque guaranteed by a cheque card must be completed in your presence. You should then look to see that the signature and the sorting code number on the cheque and the card correspond, that the cheque is dated before the expiry date of the card and the amount of the cheque is less than the limit shown on the cheque card. You then write the card number on the back of the cheque, return the card to the customer and store the cheque safely, as instructed.

Competence Builder 7

(Elements 20.2 20.3, 20.4, 22.2)

a) Unless you are already responsible for processing cash and cheque payments ask to shadow someone else doing so, or carry out this work under supervision. You should aim to become competent in:

- ▶ Counting and checking the cash received and giving change.
- ▶ Checking the validity of presented cheques.
- ▶ Checking that the amount payable is within the cheque card limit.
- ▶ Preparing and issuing receipts.
- ▶ Balancing total receipts against records.
- ▶ Cashing up and completing the necessary paperwork.

Your competence should include identifying any discrepancies and dealing with them according to laid-down procedures, and following security procedures at all times. Any records which you have to complete should always be up-to-date, legible and accurate.

b) Discuss with your boss, tutor, or the person you are shadowing or being supervised by, how you should deal with:

- ▶ an out-of-date cheque card;
- ▶ an incomplete or wrongly-completed cheque;
- ▶ a request for credit;
- ▶ a customer who has overspent on his or her credit limit.

Payment by Credit Card

When a customer offers a credit card as a means of payment you must look to see that the card is not out-of-date. You may also have to carry out other procedures, for example, check a stop list or confirm availability of credit where the sum of money involved is large.

The manner in which you handle credit card transactions will vary according to the equipment available. In some cases this is linked to the till and prints the document which the customer signs. You then only have to check that the customer's signature on the printed document matches that on the credit card. In many cases, however, you still have to write on a set of vouchers, the date, a description of the goods and the amount of money. There are boxes on the vouchers for other details but these are not always completed and you must find out what is required by your organisation.

The vouchers, together with the customer's credit card, are then placed in an imprinter. This is a piece of equipment which is simple to operate and which makes an impression on the set of vouchers of your organisation's number, name and address, and the cardholder's name, number and period of validity of the card. You ask the customer to sign in the appropriate box and compare the signature with that on the card. You then check to ensure that the impressions are clear on all copies of the voucher, return the card to the customer, together with the top copy of the voucher, and store the other copies as instructed.

Competence Builder 8
(Element 20.2)

a) Find out, and make a note of, the procedures for dealing with credit card payments in your organisation including what to do if a credit card offered to you:

  ▶ appears on a stop list;

  ▶ is out-of-date.

b) Ask for opportunities to deal with credit card transactions or to shadow the person who normally handles these.

c) If a real situation is not possible then in a realistic simulation receive and record payments (cash, cheque and credit card) and issue receipts for some form of remunerated service, such as photocopying, typing, telephone/telex/fax, or garage services; the sale of books, pamphlets or souvenirs; or payments such as those for insurance.

PREPARING FOR ROUTINE BANKING TRANSACTIONS

Paying-in and making withdrawals are the twin aspects of this competence. In addition to being competent in handling the banking transactions, you must also be able to give a reasoned explanation for security procedures to be taken in relation to transferring monies to and from the bank.

Paying-In

Payments into a bank account can be made either by using loose slips or preferably, since it provides a more easily kept, permanent record, a paying-in book of slips. Details of what is being paid in (cheques, postal orders or cash) plus the name of the organisation (the bank's customer) and account details are recorded on the slip and also on a counterfoil. The bank clerk retains the slip, and initials and stamps the counterfoil. This supports the debit entries in the organisation's cash book.

The cash book is the place where an organisation's dealings with its bank are recorded in the same way as the personal accounts in the sales and purchases ledgers record dealings with debtors (people on whose ledger accounts there are debit balances) and creditors (people whose ledger accounts have a credit balance). So long as the organisation's cash book shows a debit balance on the bank account, the bank is one of its debtors. Since the bank is a debtor in its customer's books, the customers must be creditors in the bank's books. However, if a bank's customers owe money to it, for example, they may have an overdraft, then the position is reversed.

Competence Builder 9

(Elements 20.2, 20.3)

a)   i) Obtain some blank paying-in slips and complete these after agreeing with your boss or tutor appropriate amounts (covering cash, postal orders and cheques) to record as being paid in.

   ii) Find out what you should do if:

   ▶ one of the postal orders is out-of-date;

   ▶ one of the cheques is incomplete.

b) Find out within your organisation, or from a bank:
   i) how credit card payments are turned into cash;
   ii) what you should do if a poor signature on a credit card voucher had slipped through at the time of payment.

c) What does the term bagging-up mean?

d) In a real situation or realistic simulation count and check cash, cheques and postal orders, and prepare paying-in slips. Complete other records as required. Whether in a real situation or realistic simulation follow laid-down procedures with regard to the tasks, the security of money and information, and in the event of any discrepancies being identified.

Withdrawals

If required to draw cash from the bank for your organisation you would normally do this by presenting a cheque made payable to cash. A crossed cheque can be used provided it is to be presented at the branch where the account is held.

If it is a simple case of cash being needed it might not matter what value notes or coins make up the amount. If the money is to be used, however, for making a number of cash payments of known amounts, to provide a till float or to top-up a petty cash imprest, then it might be necessary to specify exactly the value of the notes and coins required.

Cash analysis

Cash analysis is prepared to show the bank clerk the values and quantity of notes and coins required. If the money is for known cash payments it is normally obtained in notes and coins of as large a value as practical. A simple example of cash analysis is shown below.

£	£10	£5	£1	50p	20p	10p	5p	2p	1p
20.69	2			1		1	1	2	
13.75	1		3	1	1		1		
7.13		1	2			1		1	1
25.98	2	1		1	2		1	1	1
4.89			4	1	1	1	1	2	
15.34	1	1			1	1		2	
87.78	6	3	9	4	5	4	4	8	2

Competence Builder 10

(Elements 19.1, 20.3, 22.2)

a) Make out a cash analysis, showing what you will collect from the bank in order to make the following cash payments: £10.24, £7.35, £6.68, £12.12, £21.41, £35.53, £17.76, £16.87, £26.99. Ask your boss, tutor or a colleague who is familiar with cash analysis, to check this for you.

b) In a real situation or realistic simulation, carry out a number of cash analyses in order to practise and then prove your competence.

c) Discuss with your boss or tutor what you would do if the bank had not met the requirements of your cash analysis. How could this happen?

d) Take two photocopies of a blank cheque, including the counterfoil. Make these out as though you are obtaining money to meet the requirements of the cash analysis example given, and the cash analysis you carried out in a).

e) Find out how you would obtain foreign currency from the bank, including any documents you might have to produce. Is it necessary to give notice of your requirements to the bank used by your organisation? If so, could you obtain urgently required foreign currency from anywhere else? If so, from where?

MAKING PAYMENTS TO SUPPLIERS AND OTHERS

Before meeting requests for payment, for example, invoices, you must check that the financial calculations on the documents presented are accurate and that your organisation's procedures for the authorisation of payment have been met. In so doing you will find it helpful to be aware of where discrepancies arise (for example, invoices and credit notes do not reconcile to statement) and know the most likely causes of error (for example, in calculating VAT). You need also to know to whom you should report any discrepancies and errors which you identify.

Competence Builder 11

(Elements 20.4, 21.1)

a) Find out from your boss, tutor or a more experienced colleague, what the most common calculating errors are on the business documents received in your organisation, and where discrepancies most often arise.

b) If you do not already know, find out your organisation's procedures for the authorisation of payments.

c) In real situations or realistic simulations check a variety of payment requests in accordance with the procedures laid down by your organisation. These should include checking that the documents are correct and authorised for payment. You should be required to deal with a number of contingencies including:

▶ unauthorised requests for payment;

▶ invoices and credit notes not reconciling to statement;

▶ errors in the calculations, including those for VAT.

After the documents requesting payment have been checked and found to be correct, arrangements are put in hand for the payments to be made. This can be by a variety of methods. A common method is by cheque and you might be required to prepare these ready for the signature of an authorised person, plus the envelopes in which they are to be dispatched. In doing so, remember also to complete the cheque counterfoil. Remittance advices are prepared for dispatch with the payments, if applicable. You should always use your organisation's recognised systems and documentation and, since payments have often to be made within defined time constraints, you must plan and organise your work so as to meet any deadlines.

Competence Builder 12

(Elements 20.4, 21.1, 21.2)

a) In real situations or realistic simulations make payments for the requests checked in Competence Builder 11c) or a similar batch of requests. Follow your organisation's procedures and recording systems/documentation. Ensure that the payments are dispatched to the correct recipient/location, to meet given deadlines.

b) Find out about, and make notes on, discounts. Does your organisation give or receive any? If so, what conditions must be fulfilled for these to be allowed?

c) If you have used manual systems in this unit find out about, and make notes on, computerised ones.

Processing Documents Relating to Goods and Services

Much commercial paperwork and, therefore, much of what you might find yourself processing, is to do with the purchase and supply of goods and services. Some of the most common tasks are those concerned with:

▶ ordering office goods and services;

▶ reconciling incoming invoices for payment;

▶ processing expenses claims for payment; and

▶ preparing and dispatching quotations, invoices and statements.

The first three relate to the purchase, and the last to the supply, of goods and services by an organisation.

DEPARTMENTAL FUNCTIONS

It will help you in working towards competence in the above tasks to know the functions of the purchasing and sales departments (since it is as a result of their work that the documents become necessary); and of the accounts department (since this has to deal with payments in and out of the organisation). Although the functions are common, you must recognise that organisations vary greatly and the purchasing, sales and accounts functions may be split up quite differently in your own organisation.

The Purchasing Department

This department:

▶ Maintains records of equipment and supplies in use; where they were bought and when, plus notes regarding prices, discounts and delivery times required.

▶ Keeps up-to-date files of suppliers' catalogues and price lists.

▶ Receives from other departments purchase requisitions requiring goods or services to be obtained on their behalf.

▶ Places orders with suppliers. These include routine orders to regular suppliers, and the sending out of enquiries when a change of supplier is considered or the item has not been purchased previously. When quotations are received, the department requiring the item is advised of what is available, makes a decision and the purchasing department places the order. A copy of the order is sent to the accounts department to advise them that in due course a supplier's invoice will be received for payment.

▶ Keeps a check on delivery of the goods or services in order to ensure that supplier's delivery promises are kept.

▶ Checks goods when they are received, with the order and the supplier's invoice, in respect of condition, quantity, quality and price.

▶ Passes the supplier's invoice to the accounts department for payment if the goods are in accordance with what has been ordered.

Sales Department

This department:

▶ Deals with telephone enquiries.

▶ Updates and sends out catalogues, price lists and other information on the organisation's goods or services to existing and potential customers.

▶ Sends out quotations, or information and price lists in the case of stock lines, in response to enquiries.

▶ Liaises with accounts, production, stores, dispatch, and the sales representatives, if any.

▶ Processes customers' order documents; the work required here varies according to the type of organisation. Take, for example, a factory where goods will be in stock or have to be made specifically to meet the customer's requirements. In this example, the order will be recorded, and in many cases an internal order made out for passing on to the warehouse or factory for action.

▶ Checks or requests the checking of the creditworthiness of customers and prospective customers. This might take place in the organisation or be referred to an external credit agency.

▶ Checks the progress of a customer's order, chasing it up if necessary and advising the customer should there be a delay. If goods are from stock this work is aided by a goods issued note from stores, and a copy of the advice or dispatch note from the dispatch department. An order clerk will check these notes against the customer's order to make sure that the customer's requirements have been met. A copy of the completed order, priced, will be sent to the accounts department so that the invoice can be prepared.

▶ Deals with customer's complaints and after-sales queries.

Accounts Department

This may be one department dealing with all the accounting functions or there might be separate departments each dealing with a specialist accounting function, for example, wages and salaries. Since we are solely concerned in this unit with the sales and purchase of goods and services, we need only consider briefly the work of the accounts department in connection with these functions (see Unit 14 for more detail).

In the case of goods or services supplied, the customers' accounts are debited with their value. When customers pay for these their cheques or other forms of remittance are entered in the cash book and the customers' accounts are credited with the value of the remittances. In the case of goods or services purchased, the cheques for suppliers are made out after their invoices have been passed for payment.

Competence Builder 1

(Elements 21.1, 21.2, 23.1)

Find out how the sales, purchasing and accounts functions are carried out in your organisation. Compare your findings with the information given above and in Unit 14, and type up descriptions appropriate to your own organisation.

ORDERING OFFICE GOODS AND SERVICES

An organisation's purchasing procedures will be determined, in part, by whether or not there is a separate purchasing department. If so, then someone from another department requiring supplies will probably have only to complete a purchase requisition form. On this will be stated a description of the item required, a reference number (if any) and the quantity required, plus the name of the supplier and price (if known). This form is normally countersigned by a member of staff authorised to approve purchases. The department requiring the supplies will be consulted should there be alternatives on offer, but the detail of the purchasing process will be dealt with by the purchasing department.

In an organisation without a purchasing department, the person who is responsible for the care and control of the stock might also be responsible for the purchasing of it. Similarly the purchase of other goods and services will be dealt with by those requiring them.

Catalogues, Price Lists and Enquiries

It is common for suppliers to produce catalogues and/or price lists. If these are available in the office and the price lists are up-to-date, then items can be looked up when required, comparisons made between suppliers and orders sent off immediately. If the required information is not to hand, then telephone calls have to be made or letters of enquiry sent out. These need to state exactly what is wanted, including sizes, quantities, quality, delivery requirements etc., as appropriate. They are usually sent to more than one possible supplier.

In response, prospective suppliers will send a catalogue and/or a price list, or a specific quotation. It is normal to use a pre-printed form for a quotation, and for all subsequent stages of the purchasing and supplying procedures. This will state exactly what can be supplied, the delivery date, the price, and the terms of payment, i.e. when payment is expected. Any discounts available will also be stated.

Competence Builder 2   (Element 21.4)

In a real situation or realistic simulation:

a) Obtain information about the supply of a minimum of six requirements (a mixture of goods and services with at least two being for the reorder of regularly-used stationery items). In sending out enquiries for stationery bear in mind the agreed minimum and maximum levels for each item. Refer to trade catalogues, your organisation's records, and make telephone and written enquiries. The letters of enquiry should include full details of the requirements specified. In each case, two or three alternative sources of supply should be investigated.

b) Upon finding out/receiving the information, compare the alternative sources of supply in each case. Write a memo to one of the departments requiring an item, stating which of the alternatives you would choose and why this would be the most likely to meet the requirements specified.

c) Deal with a query such as a change in price or an item which has been discontinued.

d) Find out what your organisation's policy is in regard to inviting tenders for the supply of goods and/or services. Make a note of the procedures to follow for inviting and dealing with tenders, either by your organisation or another, for example, the local council.

Orders

When it has been decided from where the goods will be obtained, an order is sent to that firm. Order forms are printed with boxes/sections for a description and quantity of the goods required, any catalogue or reference number, the price, terms of payment and delivery requirements (in effect a repeat of the information which was sent on the quotation). As is usual with all forms used in the processes of purchasing and supplying, the order forms are numbered and dated, and both the purchaser's and supplier's name and address appear prominently. It has to be signed by a person authorised to do so. Sometimes the supplier will send an acknowledgement of the order but this is more likely when the goods cannot be dispatched immediately.

Competence Builder 3
(Element 21.4)

In a real situation or realistic simulation:

a) Complete and send out order forms, in accordance with your organisation's procedures, for the goods and services enquired about in Competence Builder 2.

b) In the case of reordered stock items, indicate on the records, in the manner normally followed, that an order has been sent.

Advice/Delivery Notes

If the goods are to be dispatched by post or rail, then an advice note will usually be sent by the supplier, in order to advise the purchaser that the goods are on their way. If the goods are being delivered by the supplier's own transport then the driver will have two copies of a delivery note. One copy is left with the goods, the other is signed as a receipt for the goods and returned to the driver.

If the goods are not inspected on delivery, then it is important that when the copy of the delivery note is signed and returned to the driver it has a statement added to this effect, for example, 'goods received unchecked'. The goods will later be checked against the copy of the delivery note which has been left, to ensure that what has been delivered is as stated. A check that there is no damage should also be made at this stage.

Competence Builder 4
(Elements 21.1, 21.4)

a) If the occasion arises in a real situation, or otherwise as a realistic simulation, draft or type a letter to one of the suppliers of the goods ordered in Competence Builder 3 stating that some of the goods have been found to be damaged.

b) Unless it is part of your normal work routine, roleplay making a number of enquiries and complaints. Whether in a real situation or in roleplay, ensure that you follow your organisation's procedures.

RECONCILING INCOMING INVOICES FOR PAYMENT

An invoice sets out the full details of a credit transaction. In addition to a repeat of the information given on the order form, the invoice also gives the total amount due plus any VAT charged. It is sent by the supplier to the purchaser; the same document being termed a sales invoice by the supplier and a purchase invoice by the purchaser.

When the purchaser receives the invoice the details must be checked against the order and the delivery note, including any calculations. Only correct and authorised invoices are passed for payment (or to await the supplier's statement at the end of the month). Any errors or discrepancies on an invoice should be reported and dealt with immediately.

If any item(s) have been found to be damaged, reference has to be made to the supplier who would be expected to ask for their return and would then issue a credit note. This credit note will state much of the detail which appears on the invoice. However, it will only be issued in respect of the damaged item(s) and is, of course, a deduction against the amount due.

Competence Builder 5

(Elements 20.1, 20.2, 20.4, 21.1, 21.2, 23.1)

a) Find out the procedure you should follow in the event of your discovering a discrepancy between an invoice you were checking and the corresponding delivery note.

b) Draft a standard letter of complaint which could be adapted for use if an error were found in an invoice total.

c) Find out about Value Added Tax (VAT): what it is charged on, how it is calculated, where it appears on an invoice and what tax points are.

d) What should you do if you discover on an invoice that the VAT has been wrongly calculated?

Pro-forma Invoices

These can be used to request payment in advance of delivery of the goods to, for example, a purchaser with a poor payment record. They are also sent with goods on approval and become payable if the purchaser decides to keep the goods.

Cash Discounts

Suppliers encourage purchasers to pay invoices promptly by allowing a cash discount to those who pay within a stated time. For example, if you consider an invoice dated September 15 for £100, stating terms $2\frac{1}{2}$%, net 30 days, then if the purchaser pays on or before October 15, the amount due is only £97.50 – the difference of £2.50 being the discount. Cash discount is always recorded in the ledger accounts, i.e. in a discount allowed account in the supplier's ledger and in a discount received account in the purchaser's ledger.

Computerised Procedures

As you have read, much of what appears on the various forms used in purchasing and supplying is information common to them all. It has long been the usual practice for sets of these forms to be printed or produced in one typing. The advent of computerised systems has further reduced the amount of repetitive work involved and these systems are now fairly common.

Competence Builder 6

(Element 21.1)

Using both manual and computerised systems:

▶ Reconcile incoming invoices, routine and non-routine, including pro-forma invoices and invoices with offers of cash discounts.

▶ Deal with wrongly-calculated discounts, wrongly-itemised goods, goods charged for which have not yet been delivered, VAT charged by a non-registered organisation and the duplicated submission of an invoice.

In order to receive the variety of experience mentioned these tasks should be carried out, over a period of time, in a real situation or realistic simulation.

Completing Records

After goods have been received and inspected they are passed to whoever requires them. Record cards are brought up-to-date for any stock items. Price lists and other information regarding supplies are updated as received, with copies of correspondence/forms being filed or passed on to others, in accordance with the organisation's purchasing procedures.

PROCESSING EXPENSES CLAIMS FOR PAYMENT

Expenses are paid by organisations for a number of reasons. These could be, for example, to employees and fee-paid consultants for travel and accommodation in the course of their duties or the expenses of people attending meetings or courses/conferences. Volunteers working for organisations such as charities, although not receiving any payment for their work, will in many cases have their expenses reimbursed.

These expenses are normally claimed by means of an expenses claim form. If the expenses claims are regular then there may be a laid-down procedure specifying, for example, by which day in the month claims have to be submitted in order to be paid by a specified payment date. Non-routine payments are likely to be less constrained in this respect, but may be subject to closer checks.

Competence Builder 7

(Element 21.3)

Find out for what purposes expenses are reimbursed in your organisation.

When expenses claims are received they have to be checked to ensure:

▶ that the people submitting the claims are authorised to do so for those particular expenditures;

▶ that the claims are consistent with events, for example, if the expenses are for attending a meeting that there was such a meeting held on that occasion;

▶ that the calculations are correct; and

▶ that if claims have to be supported by documents, such as hotel bills, the supporting documents are attached and agree with the claim.

Any errors must be identified and investigated, with any unresolved errors and discrepancies reported promptly. Usually someone authorised to do so will be required to countersign the claim forms. Naturally, only correctly completed, checked and authorised claims are passed for payment. Quite often expenses are coded according to what they are for. This then makes it simple to produce a list and total of, for example, all the monies paid out for travel to people attending certain meetings.

In dealing with expenses claims you need to know your organisation's policy covering the payment of expenses and what are the most common taxable and non-taxable expenses. You also need to remember, as indeed you must in dealing with all documents, that the security and confidentiality of information should always be maintained. You will have records to complete and it is essential that these are up-to-date, legible and accurate.

Competence Builder 8

(Element 21.3)

Process expenses claims, including those requiring records for taxable and non-taxable expenses, according to your organisation's laid-down procedures. You should deal with the allocation of expense codes, also with contingencies, including the need to investigate claims which include miscalculations and non-allowable expenses, and where the receipts are inconsistent with the submitted claims. It is preferable that you practise in the workplace over a period of time, say one month, but if only simulation is available, then it should be realistic and reflect the time factor.

PREPARING AND DISPATCHING QUOTATIONS, INVOICES AND STATEMENTS

We have so far considered the processing of the business documents used in the purchase and supply of goods and services from the viewpoint of the purchaser. We now need to look at the documents from the supplier's viewpoint, and in particular those which are prepared by the supplier, i.e. the quotation, invoice and statement.

Preparing Quotations

As previously stated, upon receiving an enquiry a supplier prepares a quotation. If the enquiry is for a stock line then it is very simple to prepare the quotation using information from a standard price list and send this out together with a catalogue or other supporting printed material. If the enquiry is for a non-standard line, something which has to be specially made for the customer, then an individual quotation has to be worked out.

If, for example, a carton manufacturer received an enquiry for the supply of printed cartons, then amongst the costs to be taken into consideration would be how much cardboard is required and how much ink is needed for the printing. These and all the other costs involved will be worked out individually for each enquiry. In the case of printed cartons the estimating of the costs involved is quite a complicated process because there are so many. It can be seen, therefore, that the work which has to be carried out prior to the actual preparation of the quotation can vary considerably according to the goods and services an organisation supplies.

Competence Builder 9 *(Element 21.2)*

a) What goods and/or services does your organisation supply? Find out how much time is involved in working out the prices at which these can be offered to customers.

b) What does COD mean in regard to the supply of goods?

Credit Control

If your organisation supplies goods or services on credit it will want to be reasonably sure of being paid when the money becomes due. Before preparing and sending out a quotation therefore, it is also important to check the credit rating of the enquirer. If the enquirer is a regular customer then this will have been done previously. All that you would have to do in these cases would be to check in your own organisation's records (the customer's ledger account or a separate index) or ask the staff who are engaged specifically on credit control to do this. The records will usually state an amount to which credit will be allowed and this must not be exceeded without further approval.

If the enquirer is a new customer then it might be necessary to contact one of the organisations specialising in supplying information regarding creditworthiness, or obtain references from a bank or another firm whose name has been given as a referee by the prospective purchaser. You would follow the procedures regarding this as laid-down by your organisation.

Provided there is no query regarding credit then the enquiry can be prepared and dispatched to the prospective customer with a copy kept in the sales department or customer files.

Competence Builder 10 *(Element 21.2)*

Using manual and computerised systems, and in a real situation (preferably) or realistic simulation:

▶ Prepare a quotation for a standard product off the shelf.

▶ Prepare a minimum of five other quotations involving, where possible, variations in types of service/supply, quantity and costs.

▶ Follow the credit control procedures laid down in your organisation.

▶ Use a calculator, as appropriate, for calculations.

▶ Complete any required records.

▶ Ensure that you follow the procedures of your organisation, both in regard to documentation and those regarding confidentiality. Discuss with your boss or tutor what can happen if confidentiality is broken.

Preparing Outgoing Invoices

Invoices are often prepared as a set, with the document laid out in such a way that it allows the price of the goods to be left off some copies where this information is not needed. A common distribution of invoice copies is as follows:

▶ One copy to the customer after the goods or services have been supplied, unless it is a pro-forma invoice (see page 114). If supplies are on a regular basis then the invoice is looked upon as being a means of advising the customer of what has been supplied on that occasion rather than as a request for payment. The statement (see later) is used for this purpose.

▶ One copy kept in the supplier's accounts department so that the details can be entered in the accounts and the staff know when to expect payment.

▶ One copy kept in the sales department or customer's file, readily available in the event of a query.

▶ One copy sent to the stores as authorisation to release goods when they are being supplied from stock.

▶ One copy (in some cases two) assigned for dispatch, to be used as a delivery note.

▶ One copy sent to the purchaser at the appropriate time to act as an advice note that the goods are in transit.

Competence Builder 11 *(Element 21.2)*

a) In a real situation or realistic simulation, prepare a minimum of 20 VAT invoices, including a minimum of three requiring transport charges, one COD, two pro-forma invoices and two offering a cash discount.

b) Complete any records required.

Preparing Statements

Statements are issued at regular intervals, usually monthly. They are accounts setting out the amount due to the supplier by the purchaser and contain a record of all the transactions since the last statement. To the supplier they are a copy of the debtor's account in the sales ledger. The following method is usually adopted:

▶ The purchaser is sent a copy as a request for payment.

▶ The supplier's accounts department keeps a copy.

Competence Builder 12 *(Element 21.2)*

In a real situation or realistic simulation:

a) Prepare a minimum of five statements, each containing a minimum of five entries. They must include the invoice amounts, the amounts paid and the balances.

b) Ensure that necessary records are up-to-date, legible and accurate.

Processing Payroll

This unit deals with three aspects of payroll processing in which you should aim to become competent. These are:

▶ processing documentation for wages and salaries;

▶ processing direct payment of wages and salaries;

▶ arranging credit transfers.

COMPLETING FORMS AND RECORDS

The ability to complete forms and records accurately and efficiently is an essential skill without which your efforts towards competence will be frustrated. This statement applies not only to tasks connected with processing the payroll, but throughout your work in business administration.

There are a number of subsidiary skills involved in the completion of forms and records, regardless of the purpose of the documents. These are:

▶ Good presentation including neatness in working.

▶ Clear handwriting and clear writing of numbers.

▶ Adjusting writing to the amount of space available.

▶ Recognising the appropriate place in which to insert data.

▶ Recognising what is irrelevant and can be left out.

▶ Correcting errors unobtrusively.

▶ Interpreting information and instructions correctly.

▶ Transferring numbers without transposing them, i.e. not writing or keying 789 instead of 798.

▶ Transferring information from a number of sources to the appropriate place on a document without error.

▶ Recognising when information is incorrect or deficient in some way.

▶ Summarising.

Useful tips to follow are:

▶ Always read through a form before writing anything on it, in order to avoid placing data in the wrong place.

▶ Photocopy or make a rough copy of a complicated form, and complete this first, or lightly pencil in the data prior to completing it in ink.

▶ Seek help if in doubt.

Competence Builder 1   *(Skills common to a large number of elements)*

Critically assess your own competence in:

a) completing forms and records;

b) carrying out financial calculations using a calculator.

Should you feel in any way uncertain about your competence ask your boss or tutor for an opinion. If you are not fully competent ask for some work which will give you additional practice.

In all your work, check that you are familiar with the procedures you should follow and the documents you should use. If in doubt – ask. Whatever work you are asked to undertake always find out what information can be disclosed and to whom. Never disclose information, however unimportant it might appear, to anyone not authorised to receive it.

COMPUTERISED PAYROLL

The exact nature of work on the payroll depends on whether or not the system is computerised. Since the payroll has to be dealt with at regular intervals and requires quite complex calculations, a workload which a computer can considerably lighten, it is usually one of the first areas of an organisation's work for which a computer is used.

The tax and national insurance tables (see page 123) are held in the computer's memory, together with the latest employees' payment records. When new figures are keyed in, the process is rapidly completed and the payroll records are updated automatically. Commercially available packages are widely used and normally provide printouts including:

▶ payslips.

▶ a summary of pay. (This is a list of employees showing the pay received by each one together with details of deductions for tax etc.)

▶ end-of-year documents, when appropriate. (These are statements for employees showing total pay and deductions for the year – presented as a P60 form – plus similar information in list form for the organisation's use.)

▶ taxation documents. (These can be used by the organisation for the purpose of supplying the Inland Revenue with required information as to how much each employee was paid and how much tax was deducted.)

▶ coin analysis for use where employees are paid in cash. (This shows the organisation how much of each type of coin is needed in order to make up the pay packets.

PROCESSING DOCUMENTATION FOR WAGES AND SALARIES

People in employment receive payment in the form of a salary, which is quoted as an annual amount and is usually paid monthly, or a wage, which is quoted at an hourly rate and is usually paid weekly.

The starting point in working out salaries and wages is the gross pay. Salaries are usually taken as one-twelfth of the annual amount due but earnings can be increased by commission (usually for sales personnel), overtime and bonuses. The last two are traditionally associated with waged employees, but are by no means unknown for salaried employees, for example, the payment of a Christmas bonus to all employees.

The gross figure for wages may be dependent on the amount of time worked or on the amount produced (piecework). In order to calculate wages based on time you will most likely be referring to clockcards, timesheets or other attendance records, in order to determine the number of hours worked. Overtime is often paid at a higher than basic rate on some sliding scale. If piecework rates are used, the amount produced will normally be recorded by a supervisor. Bonuses are added as appropriate.

Competence Builder 2 *(Element 22.1)*

How are people paid in your organisation? By salary? By wage? On a time or piecework basis? Have any payments, such as commission, to be taken into consideration when working out each person's gross pay?

When a person's gross pay has been determined a number of deductions are then made. Some of these are compulsory, such as income tax and national insurance (which provides money for unemployment, sickness payments, government pensions, maternity benefits etc.). Some are voluntary and may include Save As You Earn (SAYE), trade union dues and contributory pension fund payments.

Pay As You Earn (PAYE)

Pay As You Earn (PAYE) is the system used for working out and collecting income tax from pay. Under this system the employee pays tax when the money is earned. PAYE is applied to all those employed, regardless of age, who receive an earned income which exceeds the allowable tax-free reliefs. PAYE tax is worked out and deducted from all sorts of payments including: earnings, salaries, wages, fees, overtime, bonuses, commission, pensions, perks, honoraria, sick pay, statutory sick pay, maternity pay, statutory maternity pay, vouchers which can be exchanged for cash or meals (luncheon vouchers), round sum expenses allowances, payments from profit-sharing schemes, holiday pay and certain expenses payments.

Competence Builder 3 *(Element 22.1)*

Do you understand what is meant by all of the items listed from which PAYE deductions must be made? If not find out.

Under the PAYE system action must be taken:

▶ each time an employee is paid;

▶ at the end of each tax month;

▶ at the end of the tax year;

▶ when an employee leaves.

Each Time an Employee is Paid

The tax due is worked out using the employer's code number – this represents the employee's income tax allowance – and the tax tables provided by the Inland Revenue. You do this by:

▶ Working out the employee's gross pay.

▶ Working out how much of the pay the employee has to pay tax on. This is called the taxable pay and you find out how much this is from the employee's code and PAYE Tax Tables A (Free Pay Tables).

▶ Working out the tax the employee has to pay. This can be found out by using PAYE Tax Tables B to D (Taxable Pay Tables).

The following must be recorded each time an employee is paid:

▶ the employee's pay including Statutory Sick Pay (SSP) and Statutory Maternity Pay (SMP);

▶ the tax deducted from the employee's pay, or as can happen, the tax refunded;

▶ National Insurance contributions (NIC), taken from the NIC tables, and listing separately:
   a) earnings on which employee's contributions are payable at one of the standard rates;
   b) total of employee's and employer's contributions payable;
   c) employee's contributions payable;
   d) earnings for an employee, in contracted-out employment, paying at one of the standard rates;
   e) employee's contributions at the contracted-out rate included in c);
   f) Statutory Sick Pay payments;
   g) Statutory Maternity Pay payments;

This record can be made:

▶ on paper – usually on form P11, the official deductions working sheet;

▶ on computer – as part of a computerised payroll system.

Competence Builder 4

(Element 22.1)

Unless you are already familiar with it ask your boss or tutor to work through with you the procedure used in your organisation to ensure that PAYE is applied in accordance with the rules. Ask, in particular, to be shown how to determine NIC, and how attachment of earnings, SSP, SMP and holiday pay are dealt with.

At the End of Each Tax Month

Within 14 days of the end of a tax month, all the money collected in PAYE and NIC must be paid to the Inland Revenue. A payslip must be sent with this payment showing how the total is made up between tax and NIC.

At the End of Each Tax Year

By 19 April each year, but not before 5 April (the end of the tax year), an employer must send to HM Inspector of Taxes a return (form P14) for each employee from whom deductions have been taken at any time during the tax year. The return has to include details of:

▶ the employee's total pay for the year;

▶ the total tax deducted from, or refunded to, the employee in the year;

▶ details regarding the employee's NIC;

▶ the total SSP payments made to the employee in the year;

▶ the total SMP payments made to the employee in the year;

In addition, a form P60 is given to each employee.

When an Employee Leaves

In most cases a form P45 is completed when an employee leaves an organisation. This shows the employee's pay and tax position for the year to date and it is in three parts. Part 1 is sent to the tax office, and Parts 2 and 3 are given to the employee. Parts 2 and 3, in turn, are given to the new employer who keeps Part 2 for reference and sends Part 3 to the tax office. If for any reason a new employee fails to produce the two parts of the P45 then the employer sends form P46 to the tax office.

Competence Builder 5

(Element 22.1)

Unless you have dealt with them already, ask your boss or tutor to show you the various tax forms and tables mentioned and, if appropriate at this stage, give you opportunities to deal with them.

The exact manner in which you can prove your competence in processing the documentation for wages and salaries will depend upon your work/study circumstances. Ideally, you should be doing this work over a period of time in the workplace. If this is not possible then realistic simulation is acceptable, in which case competence must be demonstrated in relation to a payroll of 20 employees on at least four separate occasions. This applies also to processing the direct payment of wages and salaries (see page 126). You must be competent on both manual and computerised systems, but can demonstrate your competence on one or the other.

In proving your competence you must:

▶ Calculate gross pay correctly from appropriate documentation (using clock cards, timesheets or other attendance records as sources of information). These gross pay calculations must include the payment of bonuses and/or commission, basic and overtime payments.

▶ Calculate statutory and voluntary deductions correctly using standard tables and reference books. The range of deductions should include tax, NIC and pensions, and you must deal with attachment of earnings, SSP, SMP and holiday pay.

▶ Prepare payslips correctly and within required deadlines, identifying gross and net pay.

▶ Ensure that statutory and other records are up-to-date, legible and accurate. These records must include a wages book and/or P11s.

▶ Complete all statutory returns plus individual P60s, P45s and P46s for employees accurately, dispatching them as appropriate and within required deadlines.

▶ Deal with any pay queries, handling them with tact and courtesy.

▶ Identify and deal with any discrepancies, in accordance with your organisation's procedures.

In addition, you will find that you need to be competent in interpreting information, for example, in using the various forms, tables and reference books, and in planning and organising your work within deadlines.

Competence Builder 6

(Skills common to a large number of elements)

Critically assess your competence in interpreting information (of any kind), and in planning and organising any area of your work. These are vital skills and if you have any difficulties ask you boss or tutor to give you work which will help to develop them.

PROCESSING DIRECT PAYMENT OF WAGES AND SALARIES

Wages and salaries are paid by credit transfer to an employee's bank or building society account (see page 127), or directly to them. If paid directly, the money can be in the form of a cheque or in cash.

You must know, and always follow, laid-down security arrangements, since cheques, cash, and made-up wage packets must be protected at all times. Kept similarly secure must be information regarding employees' earnings and deductions, and you must never discuss these with unauthorised people.

Competence Builder 7

(Element 22.2)

If you are involved in the direct payment of wages and salaries check that you are aware of, and follow, all the laid-down security measures. If you are not so involved, discuss with your colleagues or fellow trainees what security arrangements would be needed to cover cash from the time it leaves the bank to the time it reaches the employee. Check with your boss or tutor that you have covered all aspects.

Cash Analysis

If payment is made in cash, it becomes necessary to work out the specific quantities of coins and notes needed, and these amounts need to be requested from the bank. In doing so, you must bear in mind that people will wish to receive notes that are easily exchanged and might not, for example, want to be paid with £50 notes. Cash analysis is carried out working down from the highest note required (see page 106).

Competence Builder 8

(Elements 20.3, 20.4, 22.2)

a) Carry out a note and coin analysis for the payment of wages as stated, to the following employees:
S. Higgins £222.71; C. James £98.23; D. Hope £107.50; G. Nanjit £94.97; G. Glover £113.32; K. Chan £219.99. Take £20 as the highest note you would place in any pay packet.

b) Check that you know how to complete a company cheque ready for signature.

c) Check that you are knowledgeable regarding bank procedures and documentation, both in regard to drawing cash from the bank and in all aspects of using cheques.

You will find Unit II helpful in working through this Competence Builder.

People do not always understand why certain deductions have been made, and errors do sometimes occur. Therefore, in this work, you might have to deal with queries from employees who cannot agree the amounts they have been paid. In so doing you must always be tactful and courteous, and deal with the queries promptly. This applies regardless of how payment is made.

Competence Builder 9 *(Elements 22.1, 22.2)*

a) In a real situation or realistic simulation process the documentation for the payment of wages or salaries for a payroll of at least 20 people. Make payment by means of cheques or cash. In the case of cheques, prepare them for signature. In the case of cash, prepare a cash analysis.

b) Through discussion with your boss or tutor check that you know how to deal with:

▶ errors in tax allowance allocations:

▶ incorrect payments.

ARRANGING CREDIT TRANSFERS

Transfers of money can be made to the bank or building society accounts of organisations and individuals, regardless of what the payments are for. When paying wages and salaries this method is a great deal safer because:

▶ large sums of money do not have to be obtained from the bank or be handled by the organisation's wages staff, as is the case in making direct payments;

▶ employees do not have to carry their total pay home or to the bank, and can draw out smaller sums of money as required.

This method also takes much less time because no cash is handled – all the payments are on paper. A slip is made out for each employee showing the amount due, and giving details of his or her bank or building society account. These, together with a schedule listing all the transfers, are sent to the organisation's bank, which arranges for the individual transfers to be made. As is true with all other aspects of dealing with wages and salaries, deadlines must be adhered to. If there is any delay then the money will not be in the employees' accounts on the due dates and could cause employees problems with payments of, for example, standing orders. As is also true of all records, these must be kept up-to-date, be legible and accurate.

International Transfers

Arrangements can be made with your organisation's bank for money to be transferred to organisations or individuals abroad. A form has to be completed giving all the details needed and either the amount of cash to be transferred is handed over or the appropriate account is debited, together with a fee for the service. The money is transferred to the foreign bank named and this bank arranges to make payment to the organisation or person concerned.

Competence Builder 10

(Elements 22.1, 22.3)

a) In a real situation or realistic simulation process the documentation for the payment of wages or salaries, for a payroll of at least 20 people. Make payment by credit transfer. Three employees are working in Germany.

b) Make notes on the benefits of credit transfer (for any payments). Give examples of when individuals can find this service useful.

Maintaining Financial Records

Goods and services purchased have to be paid for, but since trading between organisations is usually on credit terms payment is not immediate. The goods or services are supplied over a period of time, and at an agreed date the purchaser makes a payment. Consequently, records must be kept by both the supplier and the purchaser, stating what has been supplied and what has been paid for. This is part of the work of the accounts departments in each of the organisations.

ACCOUNTS DEPARTMENT

An accounts department prepares and keeps records of the financial aspects of all the transactions of a business. Since these transactions originate in other parts of the organisation, the accounts department can be viewed as a connecting link. In a large organisation, the accounts department may also be large or, as mentioned in Unit 12, the accounts functions might be carried out in several small specialised departments. In a small organisation, all the work may be done by one person, possibly combining this role with other clerical duties.

Accounts work consists mainly of dealing with customers' and suppliers' accounts, handling cash flow, petty cash (although there may be a number of subsidiary petty cashiers in other departments), wages and salaries, costing (calculating the costs of activities and products, in order to ensure that the organisation is trading at a profit), management statistics and end-of-year accounts.

The information that flows into an accounts department can be used for a number of purposes and also obliges the department to fulfil a number of important purposes:

▶ To identify who owes money to the organisation and collect overdue payments so that these do not cause a cash flow problem.

▶ To identify to whom the organisation owes money so that debts can be settled and the organisation does not gain a bad financial reputation.

▶ To keep a check that money coming into, and held by, the organisation is greater than the amount going out, in order to ensure that the business is solvent.

▶ To provide management with statistics which will show how the organisation is faring and to provide a sound basis for business decisions.

▶ To provide accounts which will enable the Inland Revenue to assess the tax liability of the organisation.

This unit is concerned in general with the first two purposes listed above. They involve tasks such as maintaining cash book, day book and ledger records, and are the competences for which you should aim.

Competence Builder 1

(Elements 21.1, 21.2, 23.1)

a) Provide for your boss or tutor an explanation, in your own words, of the functions and obligations of an accounts department, and keep an copy in your file.

b) If you have any part in maintaining financial records add to a) a note stating how your work assists the accounts department in fulfiling its functions and obligations.

MAINTAINING CASH BOOK, DAY BOOK AND LEDGER RECORDS

There are a number of terms used in accounting that you need to know, in order to understand what is involved in maintaining financial records. These are as follows:

▶ **Account**. This is a record of transactions concerning the person or organisation, asset or activity named. There are three classes of accounts:

a) Personal accounts to record dealings with people or organisations to whom the organisation owes money (creditors), which are recorded in the bought or purchases ledger, and those people or organisations who owe the organisation money (debtors), which are recorded in the sales ledger.

b) Real accounts to record dealings in real things such as office equipment, cars and buildings. These are recorded in the real ledger.

c) Nominal accounts to record expenses, losses, income and profits. These are recorded in the nominal ledger.

▶ **Ledger**. This is a collection of accounts, traditionally made in a book but now more likely to be found on cards or on computer.

▶ **Credits, debits and double-entry book-keeping**. Every business transaction involves two aspects – giving value (credits) and receiving value (debits), in the form of money, goods or services. Both these aspects are recorded in the accounting records and two book-keeping entries are made for every transaction. Thus, for every credit entry in one ledger account there is a corresponding debit entry in another ledger account. For example, cash paid to John Brown is entered as a credit in the cash account and a debit in John Brown's account.

Posting. This requires making entries in the ledger accounts from the cash book and other books of prime entry (see later).

Cash Book

The cash book is used to record receipts and payments. Since it is convenient to have these separated, the debit section (for recording cash received) appears on the left-hand side of each page and the credit section (for recording cash paid) appears on the right. Each side of the account has a column to record the date the cash is received or paid, and a column in which to record briefly from where the money came or to where it was paid. The folio (Fo) columns are used to record the page numbers on which the corresponding entries can be found in the ledger accounts (see Figure 14.1). Similarly, the appropriate cash book page number is entered in the folio column of the ledger account whenever a ledger entry is made from the cash book.

Cash Account

(Debit side – payments received)   (Credit side – payments made)

Date	Details	Fo	£	Date	Details	Fo	£

Note: The words in brackets are for explanation only and are not normally shown.

Figure 14.1 Cash account ruling

It is important to know why details of payments made are entered in a cash book in the right-hand credit column. In making payments, money is being given, and in accounting you must credit the account that gives. Similarly, details of payments received are entered in the cash book in the left-hand debit column because you debit the account that receives.

Competence Builder 2
(Element 23.1)

a) Record details of all cash income and expenditure in the cash book over a period of one month. If these duties are new to you, ask for instruction leading up to your being competent in carrying out these duties in a real situation or realistic simulation. You must ensure, throughout your work for this Competence Builder and those which follow, that your accounts entries are 100 per cent accurate, that all totals and balances are correct, and that any discrepancies are identified and reported promptly to the correct person in authority.

b) If you do not know to whom you should report discrepancies find out *now*.

Cash and Bank Accounts

A bank account is used for keeping most of an organisation's money, with only sufficient to meet immediate expenses kept as actual cash on the premises. Any cash which is surplus to this is banked and whenever necessary the ready cash is topped up with money drawn from the bank.

Separate accounts must be kept in the cash book for cash-at-bank and cash-in-hand. When cash-in-hand is banked it will appear as a payment on the credit side of the cash account (because it has been 'given') and as a receipt on the debit side of the bank account. Cash drawn from the bank will appear as a payment on the credit side of the bank account and as a receipt on the debit side of the cash account. Figure 14.2 shows a simple example of how bank and cash accounts work in practice.

Bearing in mind that debit entries on the bank account show money which has been paid into the bank and credit entries show money which has been paid out of the account, it can be seen that the excess of debits over credits represents the organisation's bank balance (£3445 in the case of Figure 14.2). Notice the manner in which accounts are balanced. This procedure can take place at any time, but the end of the month is common. If there are a lot of entries in the cash and bank accounts they will be balanced more frequently. The items from the bank and cash accounts are then posted to the ledger accounts.

Competence Builder 3
(Element 23.1)

In a real situation or realistic simulation, enter transactions in bank and cash accounts over a period of several weeks, and post them to ledger accounts.

Mr Masood invested £5000 in a small shop. He paid this into a business bank account. His first week of trading was as follows:

Feb 1	Capital to bank £5000
	Paid shop rent by cheque £100
	Drew £50 out of bank to use as a cash float
	Bought stock £1500 paid by cheque
2	Sold stock £150 and banked this immediately
	Drew £75 for personal use from bank
	Paid insurance by cheque £90
3	Bought stationery for cash £30
	Sold stock £70 but did not bank takings
4	Bought stock £55 for cash
	Sold stock £125 but did not bank takings
5	Banked cash £110

These transactions are entered in the bank and cash accounts as shown.

Bank

19__			£	19__			£
Feb 1	Capital	L1	5000	Feb 1	Rent	L2	100
2	Sales	L4	150		Cash	CB2	50
5	Cash	CB2	110		Purchases	L3	1500
				2	Drawings	L5	75
					Insurance	L6	90
				5	Balance	c/d	3445
			£5260				£5260
Feb 8	Balance	b/d	3445				

Cash

19__			£	19__			£
Feb 1	Bank	CB1	50	Feb 3	Stationery	L7	30
3	Sales	L4	70	4	Purchases	L3	55
4	Sales	L4	125	5	Bank	CB1	110
					Balance	c/d	50
			£245				£245
Feb 8	Balance	b/d	50				

Note: Sums of money have been kept small here and elsewhere in this unit for the sake of creating simple examples.

Figure 14.2 How bank and cash accounts work in practice

Sales Day Book and Sales Ledger

Sales are recorded in the ledger when a sale has been made, even though payment may be at a later date. Sales invoices are entered in numerical order in the sales day book as a first step to ensuring that all sales on credit terms are recorded in the double-entry system, although in fact the sales day book is not part of the double-entry. It is one of the books of prime, or original, entry which are used for collecting together all transactions of a similar type in an orderly sequence before double-entry postings are made. A simple example of a sales day book is shown in Figure 14.3 (refer also to analysed day books later in this unit). From entries such as these, information is posted to individual customer accounts in the sales ledger, where every customer has a separately numbered account, card or computer identifying code (see Figure 14.4).

Page 6

Date	Customer	Invoice No	Fo	£
19__				
Aug 1	*B Billimoria*	*547*	*SL 25*	*114*
2	*R Higson*	*548*	*SL 114*	*276*
3	*S Clifford*	*549*	*SL 41*	*892*
4	*B Billimoria*	*550*	*SL 25*	*200*
5	*Transferred to Sales Account*		*GL 21*	*1482*

Figure 14.3 Sales day book

B Billimoria *Page 25*

19__			£	
Aug 1	*Sales*	*SDB 6*	*114*	
4	*Sales*	*SDB 6*	*200*	

S Clifford *Page 41*

19__			£	
Aug 3	*Sales*	*SDB 6*	*892*	

R Higson *Page 114*

19__			£	
Aug 2	*Sales*	*SDB 6*	*276*	

Note: The sales total (£1482) is posted to the general ledger.

Figure 14.4 Postings from sales day book to sales ledger (individual customer accounts)

Most of the entries in these accounts are debit entries which indicate that the customer owes money to the organisation for goods or services received. Credit entries arise if a credit note has been raised, (for example, when a customer has been overcharged, goods have not been received, or for damaged goods or returns), and also when the customer makes a payment.

The difference between the total of the debit entries and the total of the credit entries in the customer's account is known as the balance. If the debit entries add up to more than the credit entries then this is a debit balance and the customer owes that amount of money. If the credit entries add up to more than the debit entries then this is a credit balance; that is money is held for the customer against future purchases.

A statement is sent to the customer, usually monthly. This is a request for the payment of a debit balance, or an advice of credit held in the event of a credit balance. The statement is, in effect, a copy of the relevant part of the sales ledger account.

Since the sales day book is not part of the double-entry, credit entries in a ledger account are needed as well as the debit entries in the individual customers' accounts. These credit entries are made in the sales account in the general ledger. The posting of each sale individually is not necessary, and totals are only posted daily, weekly or monthly, depending upon the amount of business.

Competence Builder 4

(Element 23.1)

a) Find out, and keep a note of, how to deal with cash discounts allowed to customers.

b) In a real situation or realistic simulation, record in a sales day book, over a period of several weeks, details of all goods and services supplied on credit. All the entries must be supported by correctly authorised documents.

Purchases Day Book and Purchases Ledger

As with sales, purchases are recorded in the ledger when made. Purchases on credit terms are recorded first in the purchases day book – a book of prime entry. The information is then entered in the purchases ledger, where every supplier has a separately numbered account, card or computer identification code. Most of the entries in this ledger are credit entries, indicating that the supplier has provided goods or services and is owed money. Debit entries appear where the supplier has sent a credit note to indicate that money is owed to the customer.

Like the sales ledger the purchases ledger is balanced regularly to allow the organisation to check the state of its account with each of its suppliers. When the supplier's statement is received, it is checked against the invoices, credit and debit notes, to make sure that the supplier is asking for the correct amount. Payment can then be approved.

As with sales, in order to complete the double-entry, periodic totals from the purchases day book must be posted to the purchases account in the general ledger. In the case of purchases, these will be debit entries.

Competence Builder 5

(Element 23.1)

a) Find out, and keep a note of, how to deal with cash discounts received from suppliers.

b) In a real situation or realistic simulation, enter details of all goods and services received on credit over a period of several weeks in a purchases day book. All entries should be supported by correctly authorised documents.

Value Added Tax (VAT)

Value added tax, or VAT as it is usually called, is administered by Customs and Excise and is a tax levied on the supply of goods and services. It is collected by registered organisations who add the VAT amount on to the invoices they send to their customers. Registered organisations can claim back the VAT which they themselves pay. A VAT return is prepared, usually quarterly, showing the amount of VAT collected, the amount of VAT paid and the difference. If the VAT collected is more than that paid, the difference is forwarded to Customs and Excise. If the VAT paid is more than that collected, the difference can be claimed back from Customs and Excise.

It can be seen that VAT does not form any part of a business profit and loss account. All sales, purchases and expenses in the accounts of a registered organisation must, therefore, be shown net of tax. VAT is accounted for in the sales day book, the purchases day book or the cash book, and the use of analysed books helps to make this a manageable process.

Analysed Day Books

Purchase invoices may include the cost of transporting goods to the purchaser's premises; known as carriage inwards. Sales invoices may include the cost of sending goods to the customer; known as carriage outwards. Carriage inwards must be debited to a carriage inwards account and not to the purchases account. Similarly, carriage outwards must be credited to a carriage outwards account and not to a sales account. This is because it represents a clawing back from the customers of delivery charges paid to carriers by the supplier on behalf of customers. VAT is kept separate from sales and purchases accounts in the same way.

You will have seen the benefit of having analysis columns for petty cash in Unit 11. Similarly, it is convenient for the day books to have additional columns so that invoices can be analysed before the postings are made to the ledger accounts and in order to provide for the recording of VAT.

In order to lessen the chance of error you should enter the total of each invoice first, followed by the amount of the sale or purchase, followed by the carriage and VAT. Then check that the amount entered in the analysis columns, for example, purchase, carriage and VAT, equals the amount entered in the totals column (see Figure 14.5).

Page 12

Date	Supplier	Invoice No	Fo	Total	Purchases	Carriage	VAT
				£	£	£	£
19__							
Mar 15	E Bolton	694	PL 29	235.00	196.00	4.00	35.00
Mar 16	F Günter	532	PL 16	70.50	57.00	3.00	10.50
Mar 16	T Hunt	74	PL 35	117.50	94.00	6.00	17.50
				423.00	347.00	13.00	63.00
					GL 14	GL 20	GL 45

Figure 14.5 Analysed purchases day book

General Ledger

You have already seen that customers' accounts are kept in a sales ledger and supplier's accounts in a purchases ledger. The periodic totals of sales, carriage outwards and VAT collected are posted to the credit sides of these accounts in the general ledger. The periodic totals of purchases, carriage inwards and VAT paid are posted to the debit sides of these accounts in the general ledger (see Figure 14.6).

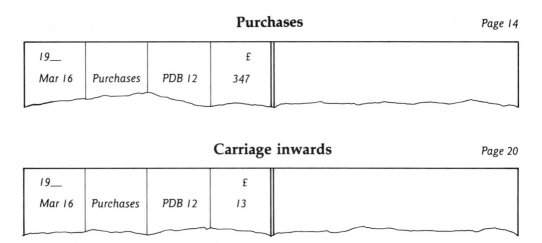

Purchases   *Page 14*

19__			£	
Mar 16	Purchases	PDB 12	347	

Carriage inwards   *Page 20*

19__			£	
Mar 16	Purchases	PDB 12	13	

Note: Similarly for VAT which is debited to the VAT account

Figure 14.6 Postings from analysed purchases day book to general ledger

Competence Builder 6

(Element 23.1)

Clarify any aspect of the basic principles of double-entry book-keeping about which you are not sure, and then make notes to use in explaining the system to friends or colleagues who are not familiar with keeping accounts in this manner.

Computerised Accounting

A large number of organisations use a computer to handle the accounting records. Computers are very fast and capable of processing vast quantities of information regarding individual accounts. They ensure that the overall financial situation of the organisation can be kept more up-to-date. Overdue accounts can be followed up immediately, and management statistics are quickly available for more rapid and firmly-based decision making.

Not only are computers faster they are more accurate and capable of updating a number of accounts simultaneously, i.e. the entries in one ledger will automatically update accounts in another if the computer is programmed to do so.

Competence Builder 7

(Element 23.1)

If you are not already familiar with both manual and computerised accounting systems then discuss opportunities for remedying this deficiency with your boss or tutor, since you must become competent in using both. If you use only one system in your workplace, you can prove your competence on the other by means of a realistic simulation, but you might need to negotiate the use of the equipment for practice and assessment.

Aged Debtor Analysis

Computerised accounting greatly facilitates aged debtor analysis. The program analyses each debtor's account and produces a printout which shows not only the current balance outstanding, but also the age of the balance. It will usually break down the balance into the amount owing from the current month, the last month, two months ago etc. This is vital information for effective credit control and gives advance notice of possible bad debts.

Competence Builder 8

(Element 23.1)

Negotiate with your boss or tutor opportunities for you to practise the preparation of VAT returns and aged debtor analysis statements.

Appendix I

BUSINESS ADMINISTRATION NVQ LEVEL II

There is a choice of three routes – Administrative, Financial or Secretarial. To qualify for a Level II award, candidates must prove their competence in the ticked units including those from Level I.

			Administrative	Financial	Secretarial
Level I	1	Filing (not a requirement for Level II – Unit 12 covers this)			
	2	Communicating information	✓	✓	✓
	3	Data processing	✓	✓	
	4	Processing petty cash and invoices	✓		✓
	5	Stock handling	✓	✓	✓
	6	Mail handling	✓	✓	✓
	7	Reprographics	✓	✓	✓
	8	Liaising with callers and colleagues	✓	✓	✓
	9	Health and safety	✓	✓	✓
Level II	10	Creating and maintaining business relationships	✓	✓	✓
	11	Providing information to customers/clients	✓	✓	✓
	12	Storing and supplying information	✓	✓	✓
	13	Information processing	✓	✓	✓
	14	Telecommunications and data transmission	✓		✓
	15	Reception	✓		✓
	16	Text processing			✓
	17	Audio transcription			✓ (or)
	18	Shorthand transcription			✓
	19	Arranging travel and meetings	✓		✓
	20	Processing payments	✓	✓	
	21	Processing documents relating to goods and services		✓	
	22	Processing payroll		✓	
	23	Maintaining financial records		✓	
		TOTALS	16	15	16

Appendix II

Unit 14	**Telecommunications and data transmission**	
	14.1 Process incoming and outgoing telephone calls using a multiline or switchboard system	Unit 6
	14.2 Transmit and transcribe recorded messages	Unit 6
	14.3 Transmit and receive copies of documents electronically	Unit 6
Unit 15	**Reception**	
	15.1 Receive and direct visitors	Unit 7
	15.2 Maintain reception area	Unit 7
Unit 16	**Text processing**	
	16.1 Produce a variety of business documents from handwritten/typewritten drafts	Unit 8
Unit 17	**Audio transcription**	
	17.1 Produce a variety of business documents from recorded speech	Unit 8
Unit 18	**Shorthand transcription**	
	18.1 Produce a variety of business documents from dictated material	Unit 8
Unit 19	**Arranging travel and meetings**	
	19.1 Make travel arrangements and book accommodation	Unit 9
	19.2 Arrange meetings involving three or more people	Unit 10
Unit 20	**Processing payments**	
	20.1 Make and record petty cash payments	Unit 11
	20.2 Receive and record payments and issue receipts	Unit 11
	20.3 Prepare for routine banking transactions	Unit 11
	20.4 Make payments to suppliers and others	Unit 11
Unit 21	**Processing documents relating to goods and services**	
	21.1 Reconcile incoming invoices for payment	Unit 12

21.2 Prepare and despatch quotations, invoices and statements	Unit 12
21.3 Process expenses claims for payment	Unit 12
21.4 Order office goods and services	Unit 12
Unit 22 Processing payroll	
22.1 Process documentation for wages and salaries	Unit 13
22.2 Process direct payment of wages and salaries	Unit 13
22.3 Arrange credit transfers	Unit 13
Unit 23 Maintaining financial records	
23.1 Maintain cash book, day book and ledger records	Unit 14

Units 1–9 (i.e. Level I Units) are covered in the companion book *Foundation Competences in Business Administration* by the same author.